LONDON BUSES PAST AND

John Reed

Capital Transport

First published 1988
Second edition 1994

ISBN 185414 146 5

Published by Capital Transport Publishing
38 Long Elmes, Harrow Weald, Middlesex

Printed by The KPC Group, Ashford, Kent

INTRODUCTION

This book will give the reader a general background into the whys, the whens and the wherefores of the London bus, a conveyance and convenience which many of the three million people who travel on them each day probably take for granted. And yet a London without its familiar red buses would seem as incomplete as a theatre without an audience, or a library without its books.

The development of the London bus and its operation to some extent mirrors the social, political and environmental changes which have taken place in London over the same period. The book traces the progress of the bus through all its principal phases from horse power to diesel power and from the vision of one humble coachbuilder a century and a half ago to the massive operation administered by London Regional Transport in the 1990s.

Since the first edition of this book was published in 1988 events on the London bus scene have continued to amaze and surprise observers. For example, who would have thought back in 1988 that within six years small capacity single-deck buses would be found working long established inner suburban bus routes, and even be penetrating the centre of London, for so long the bastion of the double-decker.

Many of the historical photographs are from the photographic archives of the London Transport Museum, 39 Wellington Street, London WC2, from whom copies are available for purchase.

JOHN REED

The front cover photograph is by Stephen Madden

Frontispiece **What was the golden age of the London bus? It may well have been the early 1930s when the General, having snuffed the competition, had a hand in developing five new bus types within three years and continued perfecting the bus body design. Victoria Station in 1933 is the scene as NS, LT, ST types and one of the new STLs (left) go about the business of moving London.** LT Museum U13179

George Shillibeer, the coach builder whose involvement in 'Omnibuses' lasted less than five years, has gone down in history as the creator of the first London buses in the form of two 20-seater vehicles in 1829. LT Museum

Facing Page **Paintings and pen drawings are our only visual clues to what bus travel was like in the very early days. This view of Bank drawn about 150 years ago gives some idea, although the strange line of men on the right would seem to be more at home in a Monty Python sketch.** LT Museum U13460.

Regent Street in mid-Victorian times with two horse buses of similar design to those introduced by the London General Omnibus Company soon after its formation in 1856. Uniforms for the conductors had not yet been introduced. Photomatic Ltd

Chapter 1
FROM SHILLIBEER TO LRT

London is full of landmarks which fill the Cities of London and Westminster to the brim. Not just the elegant public buildings but also the shops, the theatres and cinemas, museums and galleries, the markets, the acres and acres of parkland, and the river. Linking them all are London's red buses, threading their way through the streets of commerce and commercialism and out into the suburbs with their supermarkets and semi's.

The journey from the modest horse buses of the nineteenth century to the sophisticated machines of today is one fraught with problems, and influenced by restrictions and legislation at every turn of the wheel, but it is more than compensated by progressive expansion and technological accomplishment along the way.

It all began on 4th July 1829, which the history books proclaims was the day the first omnibus ran on London streets. But what influences caused London's bus history to begin on that day? A glance around London would reveal countless horse-drawn coaches creaking and lurching through narrow and congested streets. In amongst them would be small, one- or two-seater hackney coaches weaving in and out of the general mêlée. The large coaches would be full to bursting, carrying people to and from districts which, by the end of the century, would have been fused together to create the County of London — places like Hackney and Hammersmith, Paddington and Peckham, which in the 1820s were quiet suburbs still somewhat remote from the 'stones', the paved area of London, equivalent to today's City and West End.

The coaches were called 'short stages' and advance booking was generally the method of ensuring a place on board. The short stages had one major disadvantage. They were not allowed to pick up or set down passengers anywhere within the 'stones' other than at their advertised destination. A journey within the 'stones' could be made by 'Hackney' coach (an ancestor of today's taxi) but not by a short stage. The 1831 Hackney Coach Act broke the monopoly enjoyed by the hackney coaches and paved the way for the omnibus in London. But that was still two years away. Before that came Shillibeer.

George Shillibeer, a 32-year old coachbuilder, had watched with interest the introduction of a network of 'omnibus' routes in Paris in 1828. The omnibus was a new idea in urban transport. No advance booking, and running on a fixed route with passengers being able to board and alight anywhere along it, the omnibus was the brainchild of Stanislas Baudry who had brought his idea to the French capital after it had been a success in Nantes 240 miles away. It was there that the term 'omnibus' is supposed to have originated for M. Baudry's terminus in the town was by a shop owned by a M. Omnes whose slogan apparently was 'Omnes Omnibus'. By the summer of 1828 Baudry's omnibuses were carrying 300 Parisians a day.

Meanwhile Shillibeer had been seeking a licence to operate cabriolets (one or two seat open carriages) but in the omnibus he saw an opportunity. He applied to the Treasury for permission to begin a Paris-style omnibus service in London, but was refused because he would have encroached upon the hackney coach monopoly within the 'stones'. Shillibeer found a way round that one . . . literally. He planned his service to run from the Bank to Paddington by way of the New Road and The Angel, the equivalent of today's Marylebone, Euston and Pentonville Roads, which skirted the northern fringe of the 'stones'. He built two 20-seater coaches which bore the legend OMNIBUS on the side panels; Shillibeer had decided to stick with the French description, not such a bad thing when you consider that the suggested English names included 'Economist' and 'Folks-wain'. His 'Omnibus' service, initially with one coach but later with two, commenced on 4th July 1829 and ran to a strict three-hourly interval timetable, beginning at 9.00am at Paddington and 10.00am at Bank. A flat-fare of one shilling (5p) was charged for any distance travelled. The Omnibus proved so popular that within days Shillibeer's "persons of great respectability", as his publicity described the conductors, were having to turn away customers.

MORE OMNIBUSES

When any new idea catches popular imagination, there are usually those eager to emulate it in the hope that they may share in some of the glory or, more likely, profit. So it was with the Omnibus. Before long Shillibeer found himself on the losing side of fierce competition with rival operators along his route. Common sense soon prevailed, and it wasn't long before the rival horse bus operators, including Shillibeer who chaired the ensuing discussions between them, were trying to bring some order and sanity to the chaotic situation which prevailed along the New Road. By the early 1830s ninety omnibuses were plying for hire in the area and it was mutually agreed that the number be reduced to 57, operating at three-minute intervals. Control of the service would be the responsibility of inspectors at key locations along the route.

The setting up of this Association, the first of many similar bodies created down the years, and the measures it adopted to provide its customers with something akin to a regular service was not only the first attempt to co-ordinate activity for mutual benefit, it was also Shillibeer's last contribution to London bus history. He had already been declared bankrupt and, following several abortive attempts to run profitable coach services elsewhere, plus a short spell in prison following a flight to France to escape his creditors, he became an undertaker. He died in 1866 but, even today, more than one hundred and twenty years after his death, George Shillibeer is still spoken of as the man who first brought the idea of the bus to London.

The removal of the hackney coach monopoly in the 'stones' opened up unlimited opportunities for the expansion of the omnibus concept and came as significant improvements were being made to London's road network. New roads were built connecting areas which previously had no direct link between them, new bridges spanned the Thames, and many important and established thoroughfares were widened creating greater, and easier, mobility around the Metropolis; ideal conditions for the omnibus to thrive.

By 1834 there were 620 horse buses licensed in London, and the number had doubled by 1850. An Omnibus Guide published at the time of the Great Exhibition in 1851 listed over 150 different routes serving the capital and its environs. Service intervals varied from between five and twenty minutes for routes in inner London, to hourly or longer for those travelling to outlying districts on the fringes of what is now bustling Greater London. Many of the horse bus proprietors had formed themselves into Associations of the kind pioneered by Shillibeer, in an effort to reduce the competition for passengers which could, at times, become quite violent. A member proprietor was allotted certain 'times' when he could operate his vehicles on routes which were operated by his parent Association. It did not matter whether these 'times' fell in slack periods because all the Association members received a share of the receipts. The Great Exhibition held in Hyde Park in 1851 attracted tens of thousands of visitors and did much to increase the fortunes of the Omnibus owners. But when it closed business declined and forced many proprietors to sell up.

A new era of road improvements began in London in 1855 with the creation of the Metropolitan Board of Works and London's first railways were opening, bringing more people into the capital. These happier conditions should have brought a change in the fortunes of the remaining omnibus proprietors but they didn't, at least not until inspiration came once again from Paris where the art of running buses was being perfected.

THE 'GENERAL'

In 1855 the dozen or so bus companies in Paris had amalgamated into one large authority, Le Compagnie Générale des Omnibus. This not only proved beneficial to Parisiens, who enjoyed a better service, but it was a financial success as well. Three French businessmen, Leopold Foucaud, Joseph Orsi and Felix Carteret, joined forces to set up a similar venture in London, with offices in West Strand. Despite flagging fortunes, the London bus operators were not easily persuaded to part with their assets and sell out to the French, until Le Campagnie began offering up to £510 per vehicle. After this much of the opposition disappeared.

On 7th January 1856 Le Compagnie Générale des Omnibus de Londres came into being with 27 vehicles. By the end of the year the company, now called the London General Omnibus Company (LGOC), had 600 horse buses in its fleet, making it the largest bus company in the world. It was never to lose its dominant position despite some quite strong competition from new bus companies prompted into the business by an upturn in passenger traffic in the late 1850s. The new operators took away some of the LGOC's passengers, and its profits, much to the chagrin of the French shareholders who contended that the Company's response to the competition had been poorly handled. This bad feeling continued as profits still failed to rise and led to the French pulling out of the LGOC in 1859, retaining only dwindling token interest in the Company for a few years thereafter.

In the years to the end of the nineteenth century, the London General continued to expand its services and maintain its position as the leading London bus company. Competitors came and went, many being amalgamated with or bought out by the LGOC, which joined Associations and entered into traffic agreements, usually over fares or timetables, with those companies which were reluctant to lose their independence.

The arrival of the motor age in the early 1900s brought forth more competition for the General. Many new companies were attracted into the bus business by the popularity of the motor bus. By 1911 the General had taken control of some of its strongest competitors and it had developed probably the most reliable motor bus then on the road — the B-type. It wanted to strengthen its position and suppress the threat of further competition from some of the railway companies who were making noises about starting feeder bus routes to link their termini with London's main shopping and business centres.

FIRST STEPS TO UNIFICATION

We now look to London's then new Underground railways to find the next significant event in our journey towards London's buses today. The Underground railways were, like the buses, in the hands of privately owned companies. The World's first section of Underground railway had been opened by the Metropolitan Railway in January 1863 between Paddington and Farringdon. The first 'tube' railways were built around the turn of the century and their popularity had encouraged an American financier Charles Tyson Yerkes to build others. By 1908 most of what now comprises the central London area Underground network had been built and the companies, finding themselves on the unfavourable side of competition with the buses, had made moves towards closer co-operation, trading jointly under the name 'Underground'. Out of this emerged the Underground Electric Railways Company of London (UERL) which comprised the District Railway, the three tubes built by Yerkes who had also bought a controlling interest in the District Railway, and the London United Tramways. By 1910 both Albert Stanley and Frank Pick, two of the most famous names in London's transport history, had key positions in the UERL, Stanley as General Manager and Pick as Traffic Officer.

The LGOC was also busy, merging with, or buying out, its competitors; among them London Road Car, which as we shall see, had made important contributions in bus design in its early years, and Vanguard, one of the first wholly motor bus undertakings. The General also signed traffic agreements with other companies such as Thomas Tilling and by 1912 was having tentative discussions with the UERL on possible fare pooling. The subsequent agreement led to a rationalisation of routes with the General running feeder bus services to Underground stations. The Metropolitan Railway, which was to remain at more than arm's length from all talk about merger and co-ordination, felt threatened by this move and announced plans to form its own bus company. At this the UERL and the LGOC merged so they could better deal with the competition.

The transport climate in London in the hundred years after Shillibeer was very different to that which present generations of Londoners have been accustomed, with a unified fare structure applied throughout London's bus and Underground services. In the early years, fare levels fluctuated according to circumstance, both economic and environmental, and there were the shareholders to consider. It was natural for a bus operator to run services in profitable areas whilst neglecting places where, despite a social need, not enough rings could be heard from the ticket punches.

But back to 1912. In the event, the Metropolitan Railway formed its bus subsidiary but by the end of the year the company had entered into association with LGOC.

And so it continued. The Underground Group was enlarged in 1914 by the addition of the City and South London Railway and the Central London Railway. More independent bus operators merged with the General. The development of the motor bus, which was extremely rapid between the years 1910 and 1930 enabled higher speeds to be achieved and longer routes to be operated.

After the First World War, the gradual process towards unification of all London's transport continued, spearheaded by Albert Stanley, who became Lord Ashfield in 1920, and Frank Pick. They failed to establish a working relationship with the municipal tramway operators, including the giant LCC undertaking, but they rode out a storm of renewed competition from independent bus operators in the early 1920s. This at a time when men returning from service in the Great War were anxious to get involved in any profitable enterprise, and running buses fitted the bill for many. First in line of the new wave of independents was Mr A.G. Partridge who began running his 'Express' bus alongside the General's on route 11 on 5th August 1922. His open-top chocolate and cream painted Leyland bus, which was soon joined by others, was immaculately turned out and, after the General stopped trying to impede its progress, ran efficiently. The good service that Express and some of the other independents provided gave them no small measure of credence and respectability, some of which turned out to be misplaced.

But help came for the General in an unexpected form. The 1924 London Traffic Act, whilst appearing to establish the independents into the London bus pool, dealt them a blow because one of its measures set firm limits on the number of buses allowed to operate along certain routes. Although existing independents were given a share of the allocation the new regulations made the prospect of setting up a new bus company very unattractive for those still contemplating such a move. The LGOC was thus able to continue its time-honoured policy of buying out the competition knowing that others would not be rushing in to replace it.

The motor bus has very much arrived in this 1924 view of the Strand. Most of the buses in view are K-types, but to the left, on route 68, is a new 50-seater NS, then the pride of the General's fleet. LT Museum U4867.

The swansong of the independents, which numbered over 250 during the period 1922-1933 came in July 1927 with the formation of the London Public Omnibus Company which had 76 members/operators. The following year the LGOC reached a co-ordinated services and fares agreement with the Public, and took it over completely in 1929, effectively bringing to an end a colourful, if not a little hectic, era in London's bus history.

The General had been active in the Home Counties too. In 1921 it entered into an agreement with the East Surrey Traction Company, and subsequently with other bus companies including Autocar of Tunbridge Wells, and National which operated in an area extending from Luton to Romford. These companies acted as the General's operating agents in a huge "Polo mint" area around London. This arrangement culminated in the creation of the General's large subsidiary London General Country Services Ltd in 1932.

The new company strengthened the General's connections with outer London. Two years earlier it had formed Green Line Coaches Ltd to run express coach services from London to principal towns in the Home Counties. By 1933 the LGOC was providing bus travel for over nine million people in an area of some 1,980 square miles.

East Surrey's Leatherhead Garage in 1930, with a line-up of buses consisting mostly of standard General types including a new Regal single decker and Regent double decker. The bus nearest the camera is a single-deck K type. LT Museum U7413

LONDON TRANSPORT

In his twenty years in the service of the Underground Group and its predecessors, Lord Ashfield had constantly reaffirmed his commitment to a properly planned and co-ordinated transport system for London. The goal: cheap transport with the profits which came from the busiest services subsidising those which were just as socially necessary but which did not pay their way. Competition between transport modes and operators with conflicting fares made this worthy aim very difficult to achieve, but by the end of the 1920s much of the competition which predominantly affected the buses had, as we have seen, been removed. This prompted the promotion in Parliament of two transport co-ordination Bills, one by the Underground Group and the other by the London County Council, with the ultimate aim of creating a single management for their undertakings. By 1929 the Bills were almost through parliament when a snap General Election was held and a Labour administration was voted into office.

The Minister of Transport in the new Government was Herbert Morrison, a man with firm ideas on how London's transport should be developed; he did not allow the two co-ordination Bills to continue as they stood. In fact he devised a whole new structure for London's public transport with a governing Board to manage, plan and operate everything within a 25-mile radius from Charing Cross, except the main line railways which were to retain their autonomy but join the London traffic pool. The Board would be under public control, but non-political in its composition. It would have to be self-supporting because it would not be subsidised. The Labour government lasted only two years, being replaced in 1931 by a National Coalition Government which appointed the Liberal Percy Pybus as its Minister of Transport. He supported Morrison's London Passenger Transport Bill and, after a somewhat protracted and sometimes difficult passage, the Bill received Royal Assent in April 1933. It came into effect on 1st July 1933, when the London Passenger Transport Board, or 'London Transport' as it was soon popularly known, assumed responsibility for all the services of the Underground Group, including the LGOC and its Country Services, as well as those of the Metropolitan Railway, all London's tramway undertakings, and the remaining independent bus companies in the Board's area, almost all of which had passed into London Transport control by the middle of 1934.

Oxford Street in July 1936, with a good cross-section of buses of the day on parade. In the forefront is an early example of an STL, the last bus to be designed by the LGOC, followed by an NS, London's first closed-top double decker, a later model STL and an LT. LT Museum 21291.

Chairman of the new Board was Lord Ashfield, with Frank Pick as his deputy. Unification of London's transport services had finally arrived, one hundred and two years after Shillibeer had chaired the first meeting of omnibus proprietors concerned at the effect unrestricted competition was having on their business. At the end of 1934 there were 5,976 buses and coaches in the Board's ownership. During the year they had carried some 1,950.5 million people over the 2,396 bus and coach route miles within the Board's 1,986 square mile territory, clocking up a grand total of 258,199,086 miles between them. The Board inherited 1,000 buses from the independents. Most of these joined the London Transport fleet, some surviving until early post-war days.

The remainder of the 1930s were years of remarkable achievement for the Board. One of the most notable achievements was the speed with which it managed to establish its identity. It was given a head start in that the best features of the Underground Group were carried over into the new organisation; fine architecture for Underground stations and other premises including bus garages, the 'bullseye' bar and circle symbol first used by the General in 1905 (which quickly replaced the soon forgotten circle and wings LPTB logo of 1933), and Edward Johnston's clear sans serif typeface for signing and publicity, originally commissioned by Frank Pick for the Group in 1916. London Transport was soon producing comprehensive and colourful publicity with more than sufficient information about services contained in maps, leaflets and timetable books.

During the years 1934 to 1939 the bus fleet grew from 5,976 to 6,389. We can only imagine how this trend would have continued had the war not intervened. The war had a serious effect on London Transport, and especially its bus services, with 166 buses being lost, more vehicles than some provincial operators had in their entire fleets, and with countless others being damaged. And the war did not end for London Transport in 1945, for the battle to recover lasted until the early 1950s, by which time London's buses had a new enemy to fight — staff shortage.

But before the Board could rebuild its depleted and dilapidated bus fleet it was absorbed into the new British Transport Commission (BTC), created by the Labour Government which had been swept into office in 1945. On 1st January 1948 Lord Ashfield relinquished Chairmanship to former LPTB Board member Lord Latham and became a member of the BTC. He died in November the same year, almost eight years after Frank Pick who had retired from the LPTB in 1940.

The BTC years brought mixed fortunes to London's buses. The fleet attained maximum standardisation in the mid-1950s, between 1948 and 1954 no fewer than 7,000 new buses were taken into ownership, the world's largest bus overhaul works was opened at Aldenham, and the huge trolleybus fleet was replaced by the 'Routemaster', a bus designed, perfected and built in quantity during the period. But staff shortages were beginning to deplete services, and passenger numbers which had grown steadily since the earliest days of the horse bus were in decline.

By 1st January 1963 when the BTC was wound up and a new London Transport Board was created as an independent undertaking responsible to the Minister of Transport, London bus usage had dropped to 2,485 million passengers.

By 1955 almost every double decker in London Transport's bus fleet was a member of the RT family. In this view at Hyde Park Corner, a Leyland (RTL) nudges into the outside lane beside a couple of AECs on route 25. It is doubtful whether the pedestrians would cross this busy junction so nonchalantly today. LT Museum 16355.

In the 1960s traffic congestion caused serious delays to buses. This was the scene at Trafalgar Square on 22nd April 1965 and what better reference could the designers of the Routemaster bus or the FX4 taxicab have than the knowledge that you could take an almost identical photo a quarter of a century later. LT Museum 3956/R/9

THE GLC AND LRT

The 1968 Transport Act nationalised much of Britain's non-municipal bus network by setting up the National Bus Company (NBC); it also gave the Minister of Transport powers to make grants for, among other things, the purchases of buses. The Transport (London) Act 1969 vested London Transport's country bus and Green Line coach services in a new NBC subsidiary company, London Country Bus Services Ltd, while the red bus services and the Underground, remaining as London Transport, came under the financial and broad policy control of the Greater London Council.

The fourteen years under the GLC were certainly among the most eventful for London's buses. In its final years, London Transport was well and truly in the political arena with fares and service levels prominent issues in elections for the governing power at County Hall. The 1981 GLC election returned a Labour administration which had the creation of a cheap and efficient transport system at the top of its list of priorities. A legal battle with the Law Lords over cheaper fares was just one of the events which hardened the resolve of the Conservatives in central Government to abolish the GLC and turn control of its activities and services over to the London Boroughs.

But London Transport could not be dealt with in this way, and in any case it was the Government's view that public transport in London could be better served if private enterprise was given the opportunity to participate in its operation. To this end it introduced new legislation in the form of the London Regional Transport Act (1984) which came into being at the stroke of midnight on 29th June 1984 when London Transport ceased to exist. In its place came London Regional Transport (LRT), a body with the power to secure the most efficient and economic passenger transport services for Greater London.

LRT is a holding corporation with wholly-owned subsidiary companies providing much of London's public transport. From June 1984 until the spring of 1985, LRT assumed direct responsibility for operating London's public transport whilst setting in motion the machinery to create its own subsidiaries. On 1st April 1985 they came into being, one responsible for running the Underground, one the new Docklands Light Railway and two subsidiaries to run London's buses; London Buses Ltd to plan and operate the services, and Bus Engineering Ltd (BEL) to look after the maintenance of the fleet. BEL has since been 'privatised'. The LRT Act also gave the Corporation powers to seek competitive tenders for London's bus services. This new aspect of London bus operation will be discussed in detail later.

The early days of the General with a conductor standing proudly on the entrance step of a 'knifeboard'. This picture clearly shows how precarious it must have been to ride on the roof of an early omnibus, especially when turning a corner. LT Museum H7118.

Chapter 2
FROM HORSE BUS TO MIDIBUS

Since its very beginning the design and operation of the London bus has been influenced by different rules and conditions. Regulations protecting the hackney coaches determined the route of Shillibeer's pioneering 'Omnibus' service in 1829, and legislation of one sort or another has played an important part in the evolution of the bus ever since.

Shillibeer's original green and yellow omnibuses were box-shaped saloons pulled by three horses harnessed side-by-side. There were three windows on each side interspersed by panels on which were painted the names of places passed en route and the destinations. Passengers entered and left the vehicle by a rear door. Inside a bench seat ran along the sides and front, allowing around twenty people to be accommodated, far more than the short stages and hackney coaches. The driver sat on a seat at the front above the horses, level with the roof, while the conductor stood on the rear step and collected the fares as passengers left the vehicle.

The Board of Stamps, which controlled the hackney coaches and the short stages, levied a tax on the operation of all passenger-carrying coach services, the amount depending on the number of horses between the shafts. Shillibeer with his three-horse teams was paying 4½d (2p) per mile, so a trip from Bank to Paddington and back would have cost him the equivalent of 41p in taxes, more than the short stage owners with their two-horse coaches were paying. Very soon Shillibeer reduced his horse-power to two, and built smaller 16-seat Omnibuses to compensate.

The buses which came onto the scene to compete with Shillibeer in the early 1830s were built to this same basic pattern. The success of the omnibus was matched only by the over-zealous hustle for passengers by an increasing number of proprietors, many former short stage operators, whose colourful vehicles were rapidly establishing themselves on the streets of London. Paintings and drawings produced at the time romantically show the horse buses bustling with silks, mantles and toppers as people scrambled to occupy every inch of space; some even sat beside the driver or perched on the roof of the saloon behind him.

In reality things were fairly primitive. The buses had no lighting or even heating, save for straw which was strewn over the floor in winter to keep feet warm and to collect mud, or anything else, brought on to the buses by boots or buckled shoes. Despite these rather base and, in damp weather, unsavoury conditions the new mode of transport continued to appeal, although for many decades the omnibus was the conveyance of the well-heeled middle classes.

Gradually as the bus evolves we find innovations, some of them albeit relatively minor, appearing. The most interesting are those which survive in the 1980s. For instance, from the earliest days the normal method of letting the driver know where one wished to alight was to tug on a cord attached to his arm when your destination was reached, or even to bang on the saloon roof. However in 1839 a more refined method was developed by a London firm called Holtzapffel & Company. This was a bell and cord arrangement, the bell being placed next to the driver and connected to the cord inside the bus. Curiously the invention was not an immediate success, the bang on the roof approach taking many years to fade away.

THE BUS GROWS UP

By 1840 reductions in the level of taxes paid by the omnibus proprietors had enabled them to introduce cheaper fares. As buses grew in popularity more people braved the experience of riding on top, and many buses were fitted with a second seat behind the driver. Some of the newer buses had more sharply curved roofs which at busy times were used as perches by hardy male passengers sitting on the apex of the curve facing outwards. It was only a matter of time before someone built a bus with proper seating on the roof and in 1847 Adams & Company of Bow duly obliged with their Improved Omnibus. This had a longitudinal seat that was in fact the top of a clerestory roof which passengers could reach by stepping on metal rungs either side of the rear entrance. The new design had the additional advantage of increasing headroom in the main saloon. The rear platform was now illuminated at night, albeit fairly dimly, by oil lamps.

Thus was born the London double-deck bus. The new vehicles were put into service by the Economic Carriage Company, which charged half fare to those brave enough to ride on top.

There was an urgent need to increase capacity. The Great Exhibition held in Hyde Park in 1851 brought tens of thousands of visitors to London and a bonanza for the owners of the 1,300 or so horse buses then registered in the capital. Many hastily installed a longitudinal seat along the roofs of their vehicles. The seat became known as the 'knifeboard' because for some reason people associated it with the domestic felt-covered board used for cleaning knives at home. Passengers sat along the seat facing outwards, and this rather precarious arrangement seemed to overcome the capacity problem with surprisingly few mishaps.

A sharp decline in business after the Great Exhibition closed brought forth little money, or incentive, for anyone to develop further the basic design of the omnibus, so for the next few years its shape remained unchanged. More stringent vehicle checks, administered by the police, were introduced in 1853, resulting in many buses being taken off the road. By 1854 only about 800 were licensed, and those which were running grew shabby.

Happily the creation of the London General Omnibus Company in 1856 revitalised the industry, and within a few months of taking up the reigns the LGOC was holding a competition, with a £100 prize, to find a more suitable design of bus. The winner was Mr R. Miller of Hammersmith who saw many of his suggestions incorporated into a new vehicle. It was larger than previous models, six feet high instead of five with a width increase of six inches. It had a clerestory roof with a single longitudinal seat on top. Metal plates rather than rungs gave access to the upper deck.

The bus carried 26 passengers, 12 inside and 14 on top, a capacity which was to remain standard for the next thirty years. Inside, mats replaced the straw but in time the mats would be replaced by slatted wood floors. Strangely Mr Miller's design did not incorporate any new method to enable passengers to communicate with the driver or conductor.

Delivery of the new buses was slow, and many of the existing ones were modified to give more headroom and safer access to the roof area. A number were fitted with a panel along each side of the upper deck. These panels became known as 'decency boards' and they acted as a safety barrier, an ideal advertisement board and as a screen to discreetly hide the ankles of the ladies who were now venturing up to the top deck.

In 1869 the mileage duty which had long been a burden to horse bus owners was abolished. Less burdened by tolls and taxes, benefiting from cheaper horse feed and with access to new and wider thoroughfares and bridges, the way was cleared for the further development of services and the debut of new bus companies. Of these the London Roadcar, formed in 1881, is noteworthy because its new vehicles contributed to the evolution of the London bus. However its first attempt failed to capture any hearts. It was a new design of knifeboard bus with a front-mounted staircase and a front, instead of a rear, entrance. Passengers did not like this about-face approach, but undaunted the LRCC pressed on and later in 1881 unveiled what proved to be the last important development in horse bus design. This was the 'garden seat', a design featuring wooden slatted upper deck seats facing the direction of travel. The top deck was now reached by a curved staircase leading from an enlarged left-hand rear platform, itself a new feature with its origins in an Act of Parliament of 1867 which required all buses operating within four miles of Charing Cross to pick up and set down passengers on the left hand side of the road. Hitherto buses could pull into whichever kerbside a passenger desired but as road traffic increased this practice became more dangerous. Eventually the requirement was extended throughout the Metropolis. Passengers liked the new buses, especially the garden seats, and many earlier buses were rebuilt to conform, although the process took time. The 'knifeboards' thus remained a familiar sight in London until the 1890s, except that by then many had acquired a new curved staircase.

The horse bus had reached its watershed. Internal illumination was improved in the 1890s with the introduction of acetylene lamps but weight was still the main factor restricting its further development. A vehicle of increased size and with a covered top deck, which was about the only new thing left to try, would have been considerably heavier, and therefore dependent on more horses to transport it. Horse feed fluctuated in price with the seasons, and any increase in its requirement without a proportional return in revenue was not even to be contemplated in an industry which was still at that time in private hands.

In its final form the horse bus was a very different creature from Shillibeer's original of seventy years before, but although many had been fitted with brakes a horse bus was still no match for a tramcar, albeit horsedrawn, which could carry large numbers of people at far less cost because of the lower horsepower required for a tracked vehicle. By 1900 tramway systems had been established in many parts of London and, as with the buses, there were a variety of different companies involved in their operation. Many of these had been in existence since the early 1870s and eventually most of those which operated in the County of London were acquired by the London County Council, which also proceeded to extend the system.

By 1898 discussions were under way on how best to electrify the tramways. It was obvious that electrification would enable cheap high-capacity transport to be provided by tramcars to the detriment of the buses. The Road Locomotive Act of 1865 had limited the speed of mechanically propelled trackless vehicles, such as they were, to a hair-raising two miles an hour in towns, hardly encouragement to anyone wishing to develop such a vehicle to reach for pen and drawing pad. To make matters worse all self-propelled vehicles had to be accompanied by someone carrying a red flag. In 1896 the speed limit was increased to a more acceptable 12mph, and the red flag consigned to the history books.

The horse bus in its final form, covered in route information and advertisements. The scene is Swiss Cottage. LT Museum 14423

The legacy of horse bus design is unmistakable in the appearance of the early motor buses, but what a novelty they must have been to their first passengers. **Here a Great Eastern Straker Squire reposes outside its owner's main offices in Lea Bridge Road.** LT Museum 14915.

THE MOTOR AGE

Self-propelled buses were nothing new. Since the early years of the nineteenth century countless experiments had been carried out. In one of the more notable, Walter Hancock had in 1830 conducted trials with passenger-carrying single-deck steam carriages and achieved some success, but at the time no one, except of course Hancock, felt confident enough to invest in the venture.

The repeal of the Locomotive Act brought down the barriers restricting horseless carriages and numerous experiments with steam as well as electric and petrol-engined buses were carried out, and several new companies were formed just to exploit them. Such was the flurry of activity surrounding horseless buses around the turn of the century that it is probably easiest to list the main developments as they affected London's buses chronologically:

1889 A Radcliffe-Ward single-deck battery-electric bus was tried out but does not appear to have run in passenger service.

1891 The Metropolitan Police licensed a battery operated double-deck bus seating 26 (12 inside and 14 upstairs) to run between Charing Cross and Victoria. It weighed 3½ tons and, by all accounts, did not break any speed records.

1897 The London Electric Omnibus Company experimented with a ten-seater single-deck Radcliffe-Ward battery bus with more success than the previous attempts. Although the bus was never used in passenger service it made several demonstration trips and managed on one occasion to attain an average speed of 8mph! Also in 1897 the firm Pioneer ran a Lifu oil-fired steam bus for a short time.

1898 The London Steam Omnibus Company was formed by H.J. Lawson to operate a small fleet of French De Dion single-deck steam buses, but the plan did not materialise, so in 1899 the firm ordered forty Daimler petrol-engined single deckers and changed its name to the Motor Traction Company Ltd. It seems that only two such buses were ever operated, rather unsuccessfully.

1899 A 24-seat double-deck steam bus built by E. Gillett & Company of Hounslow was tried out by the Motor Omnibus Syndicate. The vehicle consisted of an adaptation of a horse bus body, mounted on a steam lorry chassis, and could accommodate 24 people. A large chimney protruded through an awning which covered the top deck.

1901 The South Western Motor Car Company operated a handful of ten-seat Daimler wagonettes in the Streatham and Balham areas, but their limited capacity meant that the revenue they earned was outweighed by the cost of running them, so they were soon withdrawn.

1902 The first London motor bus to have solid rubber tyres appeared in the autumn when the Motor Traction Company put on a 12hp Daimler double decker into service.

The same year London Road Car mounted a horse bus body on a steam powered chassis, but this strange machine was soon superseded by a Gillett double-deck steam bus.

1904 By this time two manufacturers, Daimler and Scott-Stirling, were in the forefront of motor bus development. London Road Car purchased two Daimlers, a move soon followed by many other erstwhile horse bus operators, particularly those in the many Associations which operated some of the busiest bus routes in the capital.

THE GENERAL TAKES THE PLUNGE

Few of the many and varied vehicles which chugged onto the London bus scene in the first years of the twentieth century saw long service. It was easy of course for a small operator to buy one or two motor buses for prestige if nothing else, but the LGOC preferred a more cautious approach rather than risk buying a large quantity of untried vehicles with the possibility of disastrous results. It was the era of the Straker-Squire, the Orion, the Wolseley, De Dion, Darracq, and Büssing, so the General had no shortage of different chassis to choose from. In 1904 the company

One of the General's De Dion motor buses which the company purchased in 1905. The circle and bar symbol can be seen next to the owner's name on the bus side. LT Museum A7425.

took the plunge and tested an American Fischer petrol-electric chassis mounted with a 30-seat double-deck body. The bus was not a success, but undaunted the LGOC set aside £20,000 for further motor bus experimentation. A number of different makes were tried, including a Clarkson single-deck steam bus, a German Orion with a horse bus body, a Leyland Crossley and a Milnes-Daimler. In all the General tested over thirty different chassis, available in an ever expanding market. Its first big orders for motor buses came in 1905 when it purchased 54 De Dion and 50 Büssing chassis. That year the company built its first motor bus garage at Dollis Hill.

In fact all efforts seem to have been geared towards experimenting with different traction methods rather than developing body designs, but some seemingly unimportant changes took place between 1905 and 1908 which nonetheless had quite far-reaching effects. For example in 1907 the General, the ancestor of London Transport and London Buses Ltd, decided to paint its buses in a predominantly red livery, thus ending a tradition which had existed for most of the horse bus era where vehicles operating on particular routes were, regardless of proprietor, painted in the same basic colours.

In a similar way most operators replaced the location names painted on the sides of the buses with fleet names like VANGUARD (London Motor Omnibus Company), UNION JACK (London Road Car) and GENERAL (LGOC). In fact in 1905 the LGOC had produced a circle and bar symbol which it applied to its bus sides. This was developed in later years to become the symbol of the Underground Group, London Transport and today London Regional Transport. The arrival of the motor age brought mixed fortunes for the proprietors. There was more competition which, naturally, led to another round of amalgamations. In 1908 Vanguard and Union Jack merged with the General which subsequently adopted Vanguard's unique route numbering system which had been instituted in 1906. For the first time many of London's principal routes were given numbers, some of which still relate to the same routes today, like the 9, 16 and 22.

Vanguard maintained a vehicle overhaul works in Walthamstow and had planned to build buses there. The newly-enlarged LGOC lost no time in taking over the plant and adopting it as its own vehicle chassis construction and development centre. By then it had become apparent that bus operating conditions in London required a rugged design of vehicle which could withstand the rigours of frequent starting and stopping, something which London Transport would rediscover more than sixty years later.

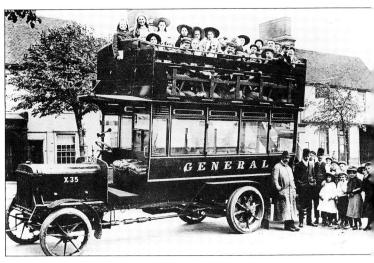

The LGOC X-type of 1909 was the first motor bus purpose-built for London conditions, but it was soon put in the shade by the B-type which was launched the following year. Maybe X 35 was giving some of these children their first ever bus ride when it was photographed. LT Museum 14911.

In 1909 the first new bus emerged from the Walthamstow plant. This was the X-type, a 28hp, 34-seat double decker. It was soon joined by sixty similar vehicles, many of which remained in service until May 1920.

For the next fifty or so years the development and style of the London bus lies almost exclusively in the hands of the LGOC and its successor, London Transport. True there were many independently-run bus companies right up until 1934, but the buses they used were types which were readily available from the manufacturers and found in towns and cities up and down the country. Many of these companies joined the LGOC pool along the way, after which established London types, in 'alien' liveries, could be found operating on their routes.

The motor age had truly arrived. For the General it dawned on 26th October 1911, for on the previous evening the last of the company's horse buses running on a route between Moorgate and London Bridge had been withdrawn. Almost three years later, on 4th August 1914, London's very last horse bus, operated by Thomas Tilling, ran between Honor Oak and Peckham Rye, ending an eighty-five year period of London's transport history and severing the last direct link between the short stages of Georgian London and the B-type, the first truly London motor bus.

THE B-TYPE

The General's X-type had been a reasonable success, apart from some design problems with the gearbox, and further development work was carried out at Walthamstow. The result emerged in October 1910 as the B-type. It weighed 3 tons 11¼ cwt (3622 kg), was 19ft 2½ins long by 6ft 11ins wide (5.85m x 2.10m) and 12ft 5ins (3.78m) high. Like the X-type it seated 34 passengers, 16 in the saloon and 18 'outside' as the upper deck was still known. The driver sat above and behind the 29.8hp four-cylinder engine. Although the Bs did not look very different from the other motor buses of the day they were undoubtedly the most reliable. Their careful design and manufacture allowed for interchangeability of parts, a quality which made for easier maintenance. By 1914 the General had 2,500 B-types in service, including some single deckers with 16-seater bodies. B-type chassis were being produced faster than the LGOC's North Road works could build the bodies, so a handful of other companies, like Hurst Nelson of Motherwell, provided B-type bodies as well. During the Great War some 1,300 B-types were sent to France as troop carriers, a valuable contribution to the war effort from which many returned to see out their days in London, days which ended for the double-deck version in 1926.

After trying out several off-the-peg types, and ironing out the problems with the X, the General found a winner with its own B type. A typical example is seen on the main road to St Albans in the early twenties. LT Museum 14897.

The first B-types were built under different circumstances to the later ones. In January 1912 the LGOC had become part of the Underground Group, and a consequence of this merger was the incorporation of the Walthamstow plant into a separate company within the Group. It was named the Associated Equipment Company, better known as AEC, three letters which were to become inseparable from the notion of reliability and quality in Britain's heavy commercial vehicle industry over the next sixty years.

Even Daimler, one of AEC's competitors, had a stake in the new company. In 1912 the Metropolitan Electric Tramways had decided to form a bus company to complement its tramway network in north and north-west London. For this it had ordered 100 of the new Daimler CC chassis developed by Frank Searle, former Chief Motor Engineer of the LGOC and a leading figure in the design of the B-type. Under the merger, the LGOC took over the MET's bus operation and, therefore, its new Daimlers. The maintenance contract which MET had negotiated with Daimler was no longer required and as compensation to Daimler the LGOC appointed them as agents to sell any chassis built at AEC surplus to the General's own requirements. This arrangement also led to Daimler supplying engines for London buses and explains why some vehicles produced before 1930 are documented as having ADC (Associated Daimler) rather than AEC engines.

The AEC factory developed a new chassis — the Y-type — during the Great War and 12,000 were built for military vehicles. Few ever found their way under bus bodies, but the high quantity produced in a relatively short space of time illustrates the efficiency and high production capabilities attained by AEC which entered the 1920s with the ability and desire to produce bus chassis for an ever-increasing market at home and overseas.

MORE ROOM INSIDE

The first significant break from conventional bus body design since the garden-seat horse bus came in the summer of 1919 when the LGOC unveiled its new K-type. The K had a larger body than the B-type, 22ft 7ins long (6.90m) by 7ft 1in (2.16m), and its construction incorporated rear wheel arches so that the 3 ton 17 cwt unladen body sat over the rear wheels rather than between them. This enabled some transverse seating to be fitted in the saloon, replacing the longitudinal side benches, a feature of bus design since Shillibeer. The K seated 46 passengers, 22 inside and 24 out. Later about 100 Ks had longitudinal seating fitted inside which reduced the total capacity to 44.

Another new feature introduced with the K-type was that the driver's position was now beside, rather than behind, the engine, a system known as forward control. The K-type thus pioneered the half-cab layout which remained a feature on buses in London and throughout the country until the 1960s. The 28hp Ks were easier to steer and, like their forebears, had solid rubber tyres, a fact of little importance since they were legally restricted to only 12mph. The Ks also had a bell and cord arrangement for signalling the driver. In all 1,132 K-types were built for or acquired by the LGOC between 1919 and 1928. The class included 24 single deckers, built in 1925, noteworthy in that they were the first General buses with pneumatic tyres.

Of all the bus types built by the General during the twenties the Ks, which were the smallest, proved most useful little vehicles when the company came to extend its services into the newly developing suburbs and country towns around London. Most K-type bodies were built by the General but some were supplied by Brush, Strachans and Shorts. Quite large numbers of double-deck vehicles were later given single-deck bodies. Withdrawal of the Ks began when the fourth generation of General motor buses began to arrive in quantity in 1930, the last K running in passenger service on 22nd June 1932.

A BIGGER BUS

The Ks were able to provide more seats for the ever-increasing volume of London bus passengers — the General carried 936 million in 1920 — but the company knew it could build a bus to carry even more. It pressed the authorities for permission to build a larger and therefore heavier bus, and in December 1920 produced the first S-type, which although in the same style as the K had a longer (24ft 8ins) body. The S could accommodate 54 passengers, 26 in the saloon and 28 on top. The 35hp engine had no difficulty in pulling the 4tons 10cwt unladen weight of the S, and the police soon increased the laden weight limitation from 7 to 8½ tons, allowing more of the type to be built. The total eventually reached 928 including 79 single deckers later fitted or built with pneumatic tyres. Many of these were operated by National and East Surrey and some of them lasted into London Transport days, but all the double deckers had gone by December 1931.

SECOND TO NONE

Most of London's buses had been double-deck since 1850, but in wet and cold weather the capital had a fleet of buses which were really nothing more than single deckers; for who but the hardy, or foolhardy, would want to travel 'outside' in driving rain or arctic temperatures? True, the bus companies fitted tarpaulins to the backs of the upper deck seats to help keep people dry should it rain, but in such conditions a bus was no match for a tramcar, most of which by 1920 were fully enclosed, or at least had covered top decks.

The Metropolitan Police were wary about sanctioning covered tops on motor buses, believing that the additional height would make the vehicles top heavy. They may have been right, and the LGOC did not try to prove otherwise by even attempting to fit a covered top to a K or S. But in 1922 the General and AEC produced a bus with a much lower chassis frame than any previously built. The lower deck was

Above **The difference between the 'normal control' B-type and the 'forward control' S-type can be seen as the wider, longer and heavier machine with the driver beside the engine overtakes B 751, probably in Ealing in the early twenties.** LT Museum 12476.

Left **All the LGOC's principal double-deck classes built before 1929 had single-deck counterparts like this 30-seater S-type saloon seen working from Leyton garage in the early thirties.** LT Museum U5592.

An open-top NS stands in the bus station specially built for the 1924 British Empire Exhibition at Wembley. The people on the upper deck could possibly be arranging to cover themselves with a canvas sheet should it start to rain again. LT Museum H9570.

reached by just one 13-inch step up from the ground instead of the usual two. The General christened the new bus NS, widely believed to stand for the Latin 'nulli secundus' — second to none. It seated 50 passengers (24 downstairs and 26 up). The new design of chassis frame made the bus eminently suitable for fitting with a covered top, and NS 1 duly appeared with one as part of its integral design. Although double deckers with roofs were by that time running successfully in cities like Birmingham and Liverpool, the ever-cautious Metropolitan Police refused to allow NS 1 to enter service in this form. The NS was thus launched on London's travelling public with little in its favour besides a lower entrance step.

The first ones entered service on route 11 in May 1923, and over a thousand had been built by the time the police relented and permitted London's buses to have covered top decks. From 1925, the remaining NS buses were built with covered tops, and eventually most of the 1,700 open-toppers of the class received them as well. The first London buses with covered tops ran in October 1925 from Loughton Garage on route 100 (Elephant & Castle — Epping).

Of course, people still got wet when it rained; the passengers as they climbed the open staircase to the top deck, the conductor for much the same reason, and the driver sitting in his open-air cab under the front canopy. But it was a start.

In its new form the NS weighed in at 6tons 6cwt and proved to be a very reliable vehicle. Twenty-five NSs built for the Blackwall Tunnel service went one step forward and one back. They had fully enclosed staircases to the top deck which, because the sides were more tapered to allow for tunnel wall clearance, had knifeboard-style longitudinal seating running its full length.

By the time the NS was in production at AEC the company, which had begun life as an exclusively London bus builder, was selling chassis at home and overseas and of course the General's associates, East Surrey and National amongst them, had some too. NSs were thus as familiar a sight in Buenos Aires as they were in Battersea or Box Hill. The last of the class, built in 1928, had wind-down windows which were to be a feature on London's buses for the next forty years.

In 1927 the LGOC took delivery of twelve large-capacity six-wheelers which were grouped into one class and coded LS (London Six). One was a 34-seat single decker, but the rest were double deckers originally seating between 64 and 70. All were fitted with pneumatic tyres, becoming the first General double deckers to have them; eventually most of the NSs received them as well. Pneumatic tyres enabled the General's buses to give passengers faster and more comfortable rides, although initially the buses fitted with them were confined to suburban services.

The giant LSs, up to that time the largest London buses built, originally had ADC engines. They appeared as AEC's association with Daimler came to an end, and as AEC transferred its chassis production to a new factory in Southall to the west of London. The new works was some sixteen miles from Walthamstow and some transportation of staff between the two locations was necessary. AEC built a special 104-seater six-wheel bus to ferry staff between the two places. It was the largest bus in existence at that time and the police only allowed it on the streets because it did not carry fare-paying passengers.

Facing Page Upper **The NS featured many 'lasts' in London bus design, including solid tyres and destination boards rather than blinds. The class did however (eventually) boast a very important 'first' in covered tops. By the time NS 1978 was photographed in 1932 it had acquired its top deck covering, pneumatic tyres and a glazed driver's cab.** LT Museum U12082.

Facing Page Lower **In 1929 the LGOC celebrated the first 100 years of the London bus. A replica of George Shillibeer's Omnibus was built and this can be seen today at the LT Museum in London's Covent Garden. In addition to regular bus services, the General actively pursued the private hire market and produced some attractive posters to publicise the facility. Much private hire was done with normal service buses which were needed in smaller numbers at weekends, but some vehicles were bought specially for such work.**

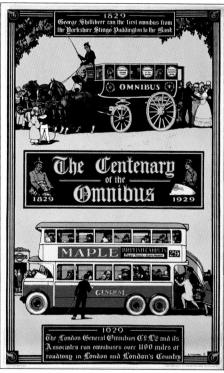

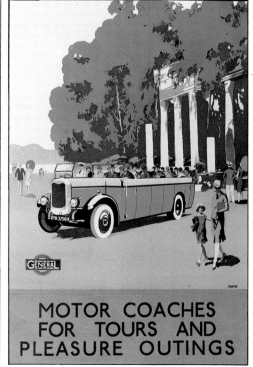

MOTOR COACHES
FOR TOURS AND
PLEASURE OUTINGS

THE LONG AND THE SHORT

In 1929 there were celebrations, for the bus was a hundred years old. A full-size representation of Shillibeer's Omnibus was built and paraded with buses old and new. These included LT 1, a brand new bus with a modern 54-seat Chiswick-built body sitting snugly on a new AEC Renown chassis with its 120 bhp six-cylinder petrol engine. It was the most up-to-date bus in the General's fleet and compared favourably with the new Leyland Titan double deckers which were in the hands of some of the General's independent adversaries. The Titan, and its single-deck counterpart, the Tiger, had been designed by G.J. Rackham, Leyland's Chief Engineer, and produced in 1927 and 1929 respectively. The new buses were quite revolutionary, having six-cylinder engines, a four-speed gearbox, and a unique chassis frame which permitted a body with a lower gangway to be fitted.

Daimler's split with AEC in 1928 coincided with the departure of Associated Equipment's Chief Engineer, Charles Edwards. Who better to fill the vacancy at Southall than Rackham, who accepted AEC's offer and lost no time in producing a new chassis — the Reliance. It was followed in 1929 by three very advanced petrol engine chassis christened Regal, Regent and Renown — names which were to be linked with Britain's buses for the next two decades. The Regal was a chassis primarily for single deckers, the Regent for double deckers, whilst the Renown was a six-wheel chassis capable of taking either type of body. By the end of 1929 the General had launched three new classes each based on the new chassis. The new buses had advanced body styling which gave them a sturdier and more substantial appearance than the NS, K, or anything before.

LT 1 (LT stood for Long Type) entered service on route 16A (Victoria-Cricklewood) on 6th August 1929. It was clad in a striking new livery; the lower panels were in the familiar red, but the rest of the bus was painted cream and lined out in black. The headlights were mounted next to the new-style radiator, one of the first to sport the famous AEC blue triangle logo.

All very modern for its time, until you came to look at the back — for there, looking very odd on such a modern bus, was a traditional open staircase, a feature which also adorned the next 149 LTs built in the early months of 1930. These were in a more conventional livery of red with pearl grey window surrounds, silver roof and black mudguards. The first 50 LTs, and ST 1, the first of the new Regents, had glazed drivers' cabs, but the Public Carriage Office ruled such an innovation dangerous on double deckers. Subsequent deliveries of both types returned to the open-cab format, the cab being designed so that windows could be fitted later should the PCO change its attitude, which it did later in 1930.

The Regent chassis STs (Short Type) closely resembled the LTs but at 25 feet in length were 1ft 9ins shorter. Both types were 7ft 6ins wide, making them the widest General buses built so far. The STs, with their 98 bhp six-cylinder petrol engines, had seats for 49 passengers. The first to ride in ST 1, which appeared in the same livery as the first LT and was first licensed in October 1929, were no doubt impressed by the fully enclosed staircase. The Regents found work with the LGOC's subsidiaries, East Surrey and Overground amongst them. Tillings had almost 200 open-staircase Regents, and these, together with other independently-owned Regents, passed to London Transport ownership in 1933 and were numbered in the ST series.

Both the initial batches of LTs and STs were fitted with roller blind indicator boxes replacing the detachable route boards used since early motor bus days. The blind apertures were small, and only permitted the route number and destination to be displayed. Later deliveries had larger destination boxes incorporating roller blinds and these were fitted either to the panel below the top deck front windows or on the canopy over the driver's cab.

The fully enclosed London bus had arrived. The front canopy was now the only feature by which it could be traced back to the earliest motor buses of 30 years

LT 1 at Chiswick Works when new in 1929. The predominantly cream livery did not last. A six wheel chassis supports a body with only the open staircase and canopy over the driver's cab linking its design to earlier days.
LT Museum U5731

A standard Regent chassis ST is posed at Chiswick works in April 1931. Roller destination blinds, a glazed driver's cab and a fully enclosed platform feature as the General's fleet enters the 1930s, which proved to be the most innovative bus design decade of all. The LTs and STs lasted for 20 years, far longer than any previous London motor buses.
LT Museum U8544.

before, and the canopy disappeared from the last deliveries of LTs and STs in 1932. These had flush fronted bodies, and became known as the 'Bluebirds' because another 'first' they boasted was a blue-patterned seat moquette fitted over a foam cushion contained in a metal seat frame. At last the London bus had bid farewell to three of its traditional design traits, the open staircase, route boards and the front canopy.

In all there were 1,428 LTs, including two-hundred 35-seater single deckers. Seating capacity on later LT batches varied from 56 to 60. The number of STs eventually totalled 1,139. Although the General built most of the bodies for the LTs and STs, some bodywork for the latter was supplied by Strachans and Shorts.

In 1929 experiments had been proceeding with diesel engines. Three STs were fitted with oil engines (as they were then called) in December 1930 with a small batch of LTs receiving them the following year. Oil engines were to prove easier to maintain and longer lasting.

The first General buses to be based on AEC's new Regal chassis with its 95 bhp petrol engine were 50 single deckers built at Chiswick works in 1929. They were coded 'T' and the class has the distinction of being in production over the longest period, for the last one was delivered in 1948. The first Ts, which entered service in December 1929 (T 1 running from Hornchurch Garage), had open rear platforms and seated 30 passengers. One of the first batch (T 38) was fitted with a 28-seat coach style body and set the style for the buses which were to be closely associated with the Green Line coach network for almost a quarter of a century. By 1938 the

T class numbered over 700 vehicles, almost all of them with forward-entrance bodies purpose-built for Green Line. The later buses, built in batches between 1936 and 1938, were classified 9T9 and 10T10 respectively. The 9T9s had 30-seat Weymann bodies and were powered by 7.7-litre oil engines, whilst the 10T10s had Chiswick-built bodies also seating 30 but with 34 seats in the later deliveries, and were fitted with the larger 8.8 engine unit. The Ts were a very stylish and hard working class, the earliest examples, albeit much rebuilt, lasting well into the post-war period.

WHERE'S THE ENGINE?

The single decker which stole the honours in the early thirties, and which provided the bang with which the General ended its 77-year existence, was Q 1. It seems that the bus was given the Q code to denote secrecy as this was the classification which the Royal Navy gave to its secret craft during the First World War. Q 1, with its 27ft 5ins long chassis, broke away from convention by having its power unit, a 123 hp six-cylinder petrol engine, positioned behind the offside front wheel beneath a longitudinal seat. This arrangement enabled more passengers to be carried. In fact the centre-door, full-fronted body could seat 37, two more than the single-deck LTs which were 20ins longer. Q 1 entered service on route 11E (Liverpool Street — Shepherds Bush) on 5th September 1932. It was joined in 1934 by four other prototypes, all double deckers based on the same side-engine principle. When new, Q 2 and Q 3 had 56-seater front-entrance Metro-Cammell bodies, with Q 3 and Q 4 being fitted with Weymann centre entrance bodies.

Eventually the Q class numbered 238 vehicles, almost all of them single deckers, built to run on London Transport's central red bus, green country bus and Green Line services. Seating capacity varied between 32 and 37 depending on the tasks the buses were expected to perform, and the body building was shared between Park Royal Vehicles and the Birmingham Railway Carriage and Wagon Company. The production batches were fitted with 7.7 litre oil engines.

LONGER FOUR-WHEELERS

In 1932 new legislation permitted the manufacture of a four-wheel chassis with a greater distance between front and rear axles. The length was increased from 15ft 6ins, the wheelbase of the ST type, to 16ft 3ins. The main advantage of this change was a reduction in operating costs, since the cheaper four-wheel layout could carry just as many passengers as a six-wheeler.

AEC soon adapted their Regent chassis to accord with the new dimensions, but the first examples to see service in London were not with the LGOC but on buses built for an independent, Charles Pickup, who took delivery of five open-toppers with enclosed staircases early in 1932. The LGOC ordered 102 new-length chassis for its associate Thomas Tilling who built the bodies for them.

The advantages of the new longer chassis were outweighed by its unsuitability to take the 8.8-litre oil engine without exceeding the new length parameters. The oil engine was already proving its worth, giving more miles per gallon and using cheaper fuel. The new buses had to have reconditioned petrol engines displaced from LTs, but work was soon well in hand on the development of a lighter — 7.7-litre oil engine.

The LGOC did not receive its first new Regent chassis until October 1932. A 60-seat body was built for it at Chiswick, and it was unveiled as STL 1 to the press in December. The new bus resembled the flush-fronted 'Bluebird' design of the later LTs and STs; in fact the upper deck actually overhung the driver's cab by a few inches making the bus look slightly top heavy. The first STLs entered service on routes 8 and 60 from Clay Hall Garage on 3rd January 1933. By July, when the General was absorbed into the LPTB, the number of STLs in service had reached 180 (although the total included those built by Tillings which were numbered in the same series).

The revolutionary **Q** 1 being tested on the General's route 11E seems to be causing some interest, most likely because of its bodywork with unique centre entrance; although its real advance was in its side engine position. Passengers were able to sit right at the front beside the driver. LT Museum 14012.

The later **Q**s had front entrances and simpler, though still advanced, styling. This post-war view of **Q** 145 shows a bodywork design from 1936.

The first batch of single-deck Regals, coded T by the LGOC, had open rear platforms, but most of the later buses in the class had front entrances and many of the early ones were rebuilt to conform. T 1 stands at Chiswick Works in January 1930. LT Museum U6059

Despite the availability of the Regal chassis, the General built over two hundred 35-seater single deckers based on the six wheel AEC Renown. Here LT 1089, delivered new to Edgware garage in June 1931 picks up passengers in Borehamwood four years later. LT Museum 18584.

The General's examples of the longer-wheelbase Regent chassis were given distinctive 60-seater bodies with a pronounced top deck overhang at the front. As with many of the specially posed photos taken by the LGOC the route information on the bus should be disregarded: STL 1 entered service on routes 8/60 from Clay Hall Garage in January 1933. LT Museum 16945.

The LGOC had long searched for the optimum capacity bus and had concluded that a large-capacity vehicle seating 60 or more, while seemingly the best option for busy routes, created fare collection problems for conductors. It was decided that a 56-seat bus was the best choice and in August 1933 STL 203 appeared with a new style Chiswick-built 56-seat body. It had a more tapered, leaning-back look, setting the style of the London double decker for the next 20 years.

STL 203 still bore the legend GENERAL on its side panels despite being among the first buses built for the LPTB; the fleet name LONDON TRANSPORT did not appear on buses until the spring of 1934. In all, 2,700 STLs were built in batches over 12 years, although the bulk of the class was in service by the outbreak of war in 1939. Each batch was different in some degree from the others and the class proved to be quite a mixed bag. The first STLs had a new-style three-in-one panel route destination layout which was to be a design feature on most London double deckers until 1978. The positioning of the boxes was altered on later deliveries and the last batches had the front route number contained in a roof-box similar to the later LT/ST vehicles. The STLs were used throughout the London Transport area. A small batch was built to low bridge dimensions by Metro-Cammell for services from the former East Surrey garage at Godstone. These vehicles are noteworthy in London bus development because they were the first to have driver's cab doors, a feature which never graced other members of the STL class. In addition there was a batch of country buses with front entrances, a small batch of 40 with humped roofs for the Blackwall and Rotherhithe tunnel routes, and a small quantity of low bridge buses for central and country bus work. Most STLs had Chiswick-built bodies, but some were constructed by Park Royal and Weymann, names which were to feature prominently in the post-war era of London's buses. In fact the last STLs were built by Weymann who turned out a small batch in 1945 that looked nothing like the rest of the class, having provincial style bodywork.

The arrival of the STLs enabled many of the older buses inherited from the independents, as well as the NSs, to be withdrawn. The last NS ran on the evening of November 30th 1937 on route 166 (Strand (Aldwych) — London Bridge).

The NS buses especially built for the Thames tunnel services were replaced in 1937 by a batch of STLs with humped roofs and other body features to afford adequate clearance around the tunnel corners. These were the last buses specially designed for the Blackwall and Rotherhithe tunnels, being replaced in 1954 by standard dimension vehicles. LT Museum 20477.

As the STLs were in production over a ten-year period there was a variety of body styles. Typical of the earlier batches is STL 442 which entered service in June 1934 and was still looking smart, despite its spartan destination display, when photographed in Romford 17 years later. Alan B. Cross.

Below STL bodywork reached its zenith in 1937 and almost a thousand vehicles were built to this general design. Ray Stenning

During the 1930s, London Transport had a contract with AEC for the supply of 90% of its chassis. Most of the remainder were built by Leyland which received two valuable orders from the Board. The first was for a batch of 75 Cub single deckers (C class) with 20-seat Shorts bodies delivered in 1935, followed by a further 22 in 1936 with Weymann bodies. The Cubs were intended as replacements for the driver-only operated Dennis Darts and other small buses in the Outer Central and Country areas. They were normal-control buses, unlike a further eight Cubs built in 1936 which were front-entrance forward-control vehicles with one and a half decks. These unique buses were built primarily for the Interstation night bus service, which linked several main line railway termini and which has survived in one form or other ever since.

The other Leyland order was for 100 double-deck Titan chassis with standard Leyland bodywork tailored slightly to STL style. The buses, coded STD, proved extremely robust in London service, lasting just as long as the STLs, and were a familiar sight on the routes from Hendon garage, where they spent most of their lives.

Left **Apart from being the longest surviving single-deck class the Ts were also the most diverse in design. T448 with its 1936 Weymann body is now preserved and was one of 50 built for the prestigious Green Line services.** Capital Transport.

Right **The Leyland chassis C class represented a break with tradition early in London Transport days, for they were the first non-AEC models of any significance to be purchased by the General/LPTB for many years. The Cubs ran in both Central and Country areas and a small batch of 1½-decker Cubs was built specially for a night-time service linking main line stations.** Capital Transport.

Leyland secured a sizeable order for its Titan double-decker from London Transport. Eventually there were 176 'STDs' which, apart from a handful with wartime utility bodies, were delivered in two main batches in 1937 and 1946. This view shows Pre-War STD 38. J.F. Higham.

THE ENGINE MOVES AGAIN

The thirties were perhaps the most inventive period of all in the history of the London bus; before the decade was over two further engine positions had been tried out on single deckers. In 1937 Leyland and the LPTB co-operated on the design of what was hitherto the most advanced chassis concept yet, an 8.6-litre oil engine turned 45 degrees and mounted under the floor within the chassis frame behind the driver's cab. Its single-deck Park Royal body resembled the then current design of T class Green Line coaches, except that the bonnet sloped sharply; the radiator was positioned at the bottom of the slope. The bus, TF 1, was the first of 88 single deckers which included 13 Park Royal 33-seater private hire coaches. The remainder consisted of 34-seat Green Line coaches, built at Chiswick. When the post-war generation of single deckers arrived in the early 1950s some TFs were transferred to country bus work. The TFs, and the Cs, remained in regular service until 1953.

. . . AND AGAIN

So where else could the engine go? Not in many other places surely, except perhaps at the back, and that is just where it was fitted in the CR type built jointly by Leyland and London Transport in 1939. These little 20-seaters had the same style bodies as the TFs, except that the 4.37-litre Cub engine and gearbox were placed at the rear of the vehicle. The 49 CRs were destined for a short life with London Transport. Being entirely different mechanically from other buses, the spare parts for them were in short supply, especially during the war, which broke out as the class was being built. The CRs were stored until 1946 when they reappeared to run mainly as peak-hour reliefs on busy services. The last ones were withdrawn in November 1953.

The legacy of this pre-war collaboration between Leyland and London Transport was the further experimentation which was carried out with rear-engine buses in the post-war years, resulting in the vehicle which was to turn the bus world about face in the late-1950s — the rear-engined Leyland Atlantean. But that was way in the future.

STANDARDISATION

In 1938 AEC had developed a new chassis powered by a 9.6-litre diesel engine, more powerful than any previously fitted to a London bus. The chassis was fitted with a surplus open staircase body from a bus previously owned by an independent and given the number ST 1140. It worked for a time on route 18C (Hanwell — Wembley Empire Pool), but was soon withdrawn so that the chassis could be fitted with a 56-seat Chiswick-built body of a totally new design, undoubtedly the most modern yet built for a London double decker. From window pillars to step corners there were no square edges, save for the corners of the roof route number boxes which were fitted front and rear. The bus was RT 1, the forerunner of a fleet eventually totalling 7,000 buses, the largest ever built for a single operator.

RT 1 entered passenger service on route 22 (Homerton — Putney) on 9th August 1939 with war less than a month away. One hundred and fifty more RTs were built to basically the same design before the Government placed strict wartime controls on bus building and allocation. No more RTs were built for another seven years. The buses which came to the LPTB in the wartime allocation of new vehicles were built to an approved Government austerity design, and mounted on Bristol, Daimler and Guy chassis. Austerity is a very appropriate description because many appeared in a dull brown or grey livery, and some even had wooden slatted seats. But they came at a time when the ravages of war were taking a heavy toll of the London bus fleet and, with the addition of suitable refinements, they gave many years' useful service with the London bus fleet. The last 'utilities', a batch of 'relaxed austerity' Daimlers built in 1946, were withdrawn in 1954.

The handsome curved lines of the TF conceal its horizontally mounted underfloor engine. Most were used initially on the Green Line network. TF 16 entered service from Romford garage in March 1939. LT Museum H16818.

The peak of mechanical innovation in 1930s bus design, the rear-mounted engine, arrived with the CR class in 1939, but it was to take another 20 years to catch on, by which time the 49 little CRs were all but forgotten. The white markings of wartime are visible on CR 9, photographed on 26th September 1939. LT Museum U30721.

The star of the 1930s, and London Transport's flagship of standardisation, RT 1, stands resplendent in its red, white and silver livery at the back of Chiswick works early in 1939. Alan B. Cross.

The artefacts of a nation at war are evident in this picture of a utility Guy (G 13), with trees and pavements dressed in white bands which have also been applied to the bus. It displays no route or garage information in this official photo but G 13 entered service from Tottenham garage in December 1942.
LT Museum U34383.

Six years of war with very little in the way of maintenance and cosmetic improvement had left London's 6,400 strong bus fleet, consisting mostly of STs, LTs and STLs, ragged and care worn. Two further years passed before the first post-war buses were delivered. Bus body building at Chiswick Works had ceased so that the plant could concentrate on overhauling, and two manufacturers, Park Royal and Weymann, were contracted to build the first batches of post-war RT buses. Delivery began in April 1947 and the first ones entered service on route 10 (Victoria — Abridge) during May. Eventually other body builders, Cravens, Leyland Motors, Metro-Cammell and Saunders Engineering, were given orders for RT family bodies to supplement those built by the two main manufacturers and keep production of RTs at maximum output.

The post-war RT strongly resembled the earlier Chiswick product except for a revised front and rear destination layout and an all-metal body construction rather than composite wood/metal, the usual Chiswick style. Gone were the rear roof number box, the sloping cab windows and the tapered rear corner panel of the pre-war model. The front roof route box disappeared on later deliveries to be replaced by a three-in-one destination display first used on the earliest STLs.

The RT body construction was such that there was an almost universal interchangeability of parts. Park Royal and Weymann had been given identical specifications and between them built 5,380 of the 6,800 members of the post-war RT family, which included 2,131 Leylands. A large order was placed with Leyland for Titan PD 2/1 and 2/3 chassis with 9.8-litre 115 bhp engines. These matched the power of the engine fitted to post-war RTs which was heavier than that in the pre-war buses. The PD 2/1 chassis were fitted with standard RT bodies but classified RTL. The first batches entered service at Sidcup and West Green garages in December 1948. The 500 PD 2/3s ordered were for a class of 8ft wide buses for which Leyland also built the bodies. These spacious vehicles retained the basic layout of the narrower RT and RTL buses and London Transport planned to use them on busy central London routes where the additional width in the seats and gangways would be advantageous. However, the police, wary that the extra inches might pose problems, refused to sanction the use of the RTWs in central London so they entered service in the suburbs, the first ones running on route 41 (Archway Station — Ilford Station) in May 1949.

When new the earliest batches of the RT family, both red and green, appeared in the standard post war livery which included cream upper-deck window surrounds. RT 2495 was one of the last to lose this pleasant feature. It is seen near Southwark Bridge in May 1955 shortly before being repainted into the plainer red livery. *Bruce Jenkins.*

The ideal of standardisation had to be departed from for some of the RT bodies in order to speed up deliveries in the early post-war period. One of the companies who supplied bodywork was Cravens Ltd, who produced 120 RT bodies in 1948/49 to this design. RT 1498 is seen on a Wimbledon Tennis special service. *Bruce Jenkins*

The following year London Transport was allowed to conduct a series of trials designed to prove to the authorities that the RTWs did not present any undue hazards to other road users. The success of these trials led to the RTWs taking up their intended duties on trunk routes through the heart of the capital from February 1951. The 8ft wide motor bus had finally come to London.

The post-war period was in many ways just as difficult for London Transport as the war itself had been. Britain was rebuilding, and bus construction had to take its turn in the queue for scarce materials. By 1949 bus bodies were being supplied faster than chassis, so a batch of STLs with premature body fatigue was withdrawn and the chassis modified to fit new RT bodies. Thus was born the SRT class, a well-intentioned measure which met with instant hostility from bus crews, because the smaller 7.7-litre engine in the heavier RT body made the vehicles sluggish and difficult to handle. Ultimately the SRTs were confined to work on routes without too many hills; a speedier supply of chassis by 1953 enabled them all to be withdrawn and the bodies fitted to new chassis, the last SRT running in April 1954. Just seven months later on 11th November the last new RT was delivered to London Transport. By that time the bus, in its familiar central bus red, country bus green and even Green Line colours had become a familiar sight on every thoroughfare, in every suburb and in every country town in the vast 1,986 square mile area served by London Transport. It had replaced almost the entire pre-war and wartime double-deck bus fleet, as well as the earliest examples of its own class and the 1,800 strong fleet of trams.

With the RT London Transport had gone as far as it would in achieving its time-honoured goal of a standardised bus fleet. It could take 8 to 10 years to replace a bus fleet the size of London's and technology cannot stand still all that time. By the mid-1950s more advanced double deckers were available and running for other British operators.

But in 1955 the RT reigned supreme. At the end of the year 6,170 RT/RTL/RTW buses were scheduled for service on Monday to Friday, out of a total of 7,048 vehicles; that is 87% of the entire fleet.

Without doubt the RT can lay claim to be the most famous London bus of all time; and so far it has achieved the greatest longevity. When the last one, RT 624, running on route 62 (Barking — Barkingside) ran into Barking garage at lunchtime on 7th April 1979 the class had clocked up a total of almost 40 years continuous service, a mobile monument to good, simple, functional design and easy maintenance.

MORE SINGLE DECKERS

To replace the pre-war single-deck bus fleet, including the vehicles running on the prestigious Green Line services, London Transport ordered 700 AEC Regal Mark IV chassis with Metro-Cammell bodywork. The order followed successful trials in 1950 with a Park Royal bodied AEC Regal. The new buses were classified RF, and the first entered service on Green Line route 704 (Windsor — Tunbridge Wells) in October 1951. Eventually the RFs found work on all types of London bus service from suburban red bus routes to country and Green Line routes. The class included 25 Private Hire coaches which, at 27ft 6ins long, were 2ft 6ins shorter than the majority of the class. The attractive design of the RF was very modern for its time. With their front entrance, full-fronted stylishly contoured bodies they hardly looked dated when the last ones were withdrawn in March 1979. The front entrance was a characteristic which made them eminently suitable for LT's first tentative steps into the realms of one-person operation (OPO) with large capacity buses, which began experimentally on country area route 419 (Epsom — Langley Vale) on 3rd May 1954. Ten years later history repeated itself when RFs, this time in the central area, were used to convert some red bus routes to OPO. By 1971 all the RFs remaining in service with London Transport and London Country were driver-only operated.

Although the RT family, and the RFs, formed the backbone of London Transport's

In 1949 the 8ft wide version of the RT was introduced. An all-Leyland product, RTW 154 is seen alongside 7ft 6ins wide RTL 684, the latter bodied by Metro-Cammell — another name still associated with London's buses today. Alan B. Cross

A gleaming new AEC Regal RF class single decker in Green Line service at Victoria. The modern lines of the RF would hardly look out of place running around London today, and yet this photograph of RF 26 was taken in 1952. LT Museum 15047.

post-war bus fleet there were over 300 other vehicles delivered after 1945 which offered little new in the way of innovation but are nevertheless worth mentioning. Between 1946 and 1948 LT took delivery of more than 200 single deckers, 80 AEC Regals and 131 Leyland PS1 Tigers. The Regals were slotted in at the end of the famous T class while the Tigers were coded TD. Weymann and Mann Egerton built the bodies for these handsome vehicles, which were to be the last open radiator single deckers delivered to London Transport. In 1950 the first of 76 AEC Regents with standard Weymann low bridge double-deck bodies was delivered. LT gave these vehicles the code RLH and they were used in both central and country bus areas until 1971. In 1953 eighty-four normal-control Guy single deckers with Perkins 65bhp engines and 26-seat Eastern Coach Works bodies arrived to replace the pre-war Leyland Cubs on the quieter driver-only operated routes in the country area.

On 1st January 1956 London's fleet of 7,000 motor buses was still in the prime of life. Even the oldest members, the 151 pre-war RTs, most of which were now being used as driver trainers, were still less then 20 years old, and the vast majority had given less than nine years' service. The award for the oldest London 'buses' still around at that time went to the 1,700 strong fleet of trolleybuses, replacement of which was high on LT's list of priorities.

The first post-war single deckers delivered in 1946 still had a distinctly pre-war look to them, although that probably doesn't bother the passengers boarding this Weymann bodied AEC Regal (T 766) at Greenford.
Bruce Jenkins

The last vehicles of the T class were bodied by Mann Egerton and delivered for country area use in 1948. They lasted in service until 1962.

The 76 low-height AEC Regents (RLH class) brought a distinctly provincial flavour to London's buses and looked rather dated beside RTs of similar vintage. Such a comparison is possible in this view of RLH 21, with RT 2833 behind, taken at Staines in July 1966. Capital Transport

In addition to the original Green Line vehicles, RFs were also produced in central bus and country bus versions. Until converted for one-man operation, the entrances on these were not fitted with doors. Central RF 365 is shown at Buckhurst Hill operating as a two-man crew vehicle, while country RFs 542 and 565 at Uxbridge have been converted for one-man work. Capital Transport

Before the minibuses of 1972, London Transport's smallest post-war vehicles were the 84 twenty-six seater Guys, all of which worked in the Country Area. One such was GS 15 which is seen at Rickmansworth in 1967. Capital Transport

RM 2 entered trial service from Reigate garage in May 1957 and is seen here about to enter Kingston station bus stand, the northern terminus of route 406 to which it was allocated. RM 2 was repainted red the following September. Bruce Jenkins

THE ROUTEMASTER

The original intention had been to build a new fleet of trolleybuses for London and consideration was given to the possibility of a vehicle designed for construction either as a diesel bus or a trolleybus, thereby making the maximum use of interchangeable parts; surely the ultimate in standardisation! However the vehicle which was eventually unveiled as the replacement for London's trolleybuses was a stylish diesel-engined bus which London Transport christened Routemaster — London's bus of the future. The prototype was exhibited at the 1954 Commercial Motor Show.

RM 1 boasted a host of new features. For example it had no chassis. Although there had been many chassisless trolleybuses in the London fleet this was the first double-deck diesel bus built to this principle. Instead the engine and gearbox, together with the coil springs and axles, were mounted on two small subframes and were easily detachable from the 27ft long, 8ft wide Park Royal aluminium alloy body built, like the RT, with ease of maintenance and overhaul in mind. RM 1 had seats for 64 passengers instead of the customary 56, London Transport obviously having been satisfied that an extra eight would not present significant fare collection problems. To keep within legal length limitations the bus had its radiator mounted horizontally beneath the driver's cab. A plain panel, sporting the LT 'bullseye', was fitted in the position usually occupied by the radiator. In this form, it entered service on route 2 (Golders Green — Crystal Palace) on 8th February 1956. The radiator was eventually moved to its traditional position in front of the engine when the permitted maximum length was increased to 30 feet later in 1956. RM 1 was now 27ft 6ins long.

Three more prototype Routemasters were built, RM 2 had AEC running units and, like RM 1, a Park Royal body; it was painted in country area green livery. RML 3 was a Weymann bodied 9.8-litre Leyland and finally there was CRL 4, a double-deck Green Line coach with an ECW body and Leyland engine.

The first production RMs entered service on selected busy central London routes during the summer of 1959. They were withdrawn later in the year to reappear on 11th November at Poplar and West Ham garages in their intended role as trolleybus replacements, a function they performed until May 1962 when London's last trolleybuses were withdrawn. After that the class made considerable inroads into the Leyland members of the RT family.

All the RMs were painted red, RM 2's brief spell in country bus green during 1957 being the only exception. The body-building contract for the Routemaster had been given exclusively to Park Royal, and in the ten years between 1958 and 1968 the firm built 2,821 bodies for London Transport, mostly of the standard 64-seat variety. However there were variants. In 1961 twenty-four 30ft-long 72-seater Routemasters were built, easily distinguishable from the standard RM by the addition of a small window in the centre of each deck. The RMLs, as they were eventually classified, were the forerunners of a further 500 delivered between 1965 and 1968 for the central and country areas. The arrival of the RMLs enabled the remaining RTLs and RTWs, plus some RTs, to be withdrawn.

Following successful trials with the Green Line coach Routemaster, CRL 4, London Transport ordered a batch of 68 coach RMs (coded RMC) in 1962. For the first time Green Line had a fleet of double-deck vehicles offering high standards in comfort, standards taken still further in 1965 with the delivery of forty-three 30ft long coach Routemasters (RCLs). There was also a forward entrance 30ft Routemaster (RMF 1254) which was used as the prototype of a fleet of 65 coaches to run the BEA service in place of the AEC Regals. These were delivered in 1966/67.

The Routemaster class was still almost intact in 1980 when London Transport purchased back most of the Routemasters which had passed into London Country ownership in 1970. Since 1982 many RMs have been sold, some for scrap, but several have found homes with new and established bus operators up and down the country, and even abroad: operators wise enough to perceive the advantages of a sturdy, reliable, easy to maintain bus with rapid boarding/alighting potential.

In 1966 London Transport produced its last own-design bus, the FRM, a front-entrance, rear-engined version of the Routemaster. By then the signals were clear: London's 'bus of the future' would be one without the traditional conductor; but with several generations of successful buses behind it London Transport considered itself more than capable of designing a suitable rear-engined bus for one-man operation. The prototype FRM had an AEC AV 961 rear-mounted engine. Its 72-seat Park Royal body contained about 60% of standard RM body parts so a large class of FRMs would have co-existed happily with their open-platform contemporaries. But it was not to be. By the time FRM 1 entered service from Tottenham garage on 26th June 1967, London Transport had already placed an order for 150 single-deck buses of manufacturer's standard design to satisfy the urgent need to start conversions to one-manning, and more were to follow.

On 1st March 1968, without ceremony, brand new RML 2760 entered service from Upton Park garage. Not only was it the last Routemaster of all, it was also the last London bus to be built with a traditional open rear platform. It is an appropriate irony that a quarter of a century later RML 2760 was still in active service at Upton Park, long after the first and subsequent generations of buses designed to replace the traditional open-platform London bus had been consigned to the scrap heap. Indeed there is every chance that RML 2760 and its peers will be carrying Londoners into the 21st century. By the beginning of 1994 over 400 RMLs had been refurbished, with new interior lighting and décor and new engines by Cummins or Iveco.

RM 1 had been the result of two years rigorous experimentation by the time this early colour view of it was taken at Crystal Palace in June 1956.
R.C. Riley

The Production RM was generally similar in appearance to the prototypes but with modified bonnet and radiator grille design. Route 52A and 25 were operated by RMs on Sundays only when this photo was taken in 1966, while route 16 was one of the first ordinary bus routes to be converted fully to Routemasters after the close of London's trolleybus network in 1962.
Capital Transport

The RCLs built in 1965 exclusively for Green Line work represented the ultimate in comfort for passengers, but within ten years they had nearly all been demoted to work on ordinary bus services because crew operation for even the busier Green Line routes was becoming uneconomic. In its intended role, RCL 2231 stands in Aldgate bus station in June 1965 next to one of the RTs the class was gradually replacing.
Capital Transport

The 500 thirty-feet long Routemasters delivered between 1965 and 1968 included 100 for London Transport's country area. Brand new RML 2310 working from Godstone garage, glistens in the autumn sunshine in October 1965. *Capital Transport*

Over 20 years have passed since FRM 1, London's last purpose-built double decker, made its debut. When it was photographed entering Tottenham garage in the summer of 1969 circumstances had already cast it in the role of a curiosity rather than the first of a major class. *Capital Transport*

PAY AS YOU ENTER

The use of driver-only buses in London can be traced right back to horse bus days, but until the 1950s they were confined to the quietest routes. Today one-person operation (opo) accounts for over 80% of London's bus services.

The problems which led London Transport to introduce large-scale driver-only operation, a programme which is still in progress in 1988, have their origins as far back as 1950 with the ending of post-war petrol rationing. Sales of private cars increased sharply, with a consequent fall in the number of people relying exclusively on buses for work and leisure travel. The resulting drop in revenue made it difficult for LT to keep its wage rates competitive with those being offered in other industries where unsocial hours, an unfortunate but essential element of jobs in public transport, were not part of the working conditions. Staff, attracted by better prospects elsewhere, left in their hundreds. While there was some fluctuation in staff shortages year by year during the 1950s, some idea of the situation can be gathered from London Transport's Annual Report for 1959 which recorded that the staff shortages for the road services operating department rose from 828 at the end of 1958 to 2,785 at the end of 1959. The total number of drivers and conductors employed dropped by 9% from 39,874 to 36,303, partly because of the increased vacancies and partly due to the service cuts following the 1958 bus strike. As reliability suffered, more people took to their cars: the number of cars coming into central London during the morning rush hour more than doubled between 1952 and 1964 to 66,000.

In 1966 London Transport published a report entitled 'Reshaping London's Bus Services' which set out plans for radical changes to the structure of London's bus routes including the introduction of a large fleet of driver-only buses to lead the front line attack against staff shortages. Routes were to be shorter and some would be operated on a flat-fare principle. All major centres in Greater London would have a network of flat-fare 'satellite' routes operated by large capacity single-deck buses equipped for automatic fare collection.

The previous year, London Transport had ordered 58 double deckers with standard Park Royal front entrance bodywork, similar to buses then running in many provincial towns. Fifty of the buses had Leyland Atlantean 11.1-litre engines. They were painted red, coded XA and used in trials alongside new RMLs on routes 24 and 76 to compare the operation of doored and open-platform vehicles on busy routes. The remaining eight were Daimler Fleetline (XF class) painted green and fitted with Gardner 6LX 10.4-litre engines. They were allocated to East Grinstead garage's route 424 and were used as normal crew-operated buses for most of the day. At that time legislation did not permit the operation of double-deck buses by just one person. However after the evening rush hour the upper deck was closed off and the XFs became nocturnal driver-only single deckers.

The other significant development was the introduction of route 500, a flat-fare express route linking Victoria Station with Marble Arch and Oxford Street for commuters and shoppers travelling from one of London's busiest main line rail terminals to one of the principal shopping and business thoroughfares in the capital. Passengers deposited 6d pieces (2½p) in new style coin-in-the-slot machines to gain entrance; no tickets were issued.

Route 500 was given the name 'Red Arrow'. To run it London Transport purchased 14 Strachans-bodied AEC AH691 Swifts, which LT christened 'Merlin'. They were designed to move large numbers of short distance riders at busy times and had a carrying capacity of 73 (25 seated and 48 standing). Those who ventured aboard route 500 did not seem to find the experience too arduous, the service being hailed as an unqualified success. The 500 was the first route in a network of 'Red Arrows' centred on London's principal main line railway termini, a network which thrives today.

London Transport seemed satisfied with the Merlins, for in 1967 it placed large orders for similar buses, this time with Metro-Cammell Weymann bodywork, for use in the initial stages of its mammoth Bus Reshaping Programme. Eventually 665 were delivered with quantities for central and country area routes.

The first MBs, as the class was collectively called, arrived in the autumn of 1967. The buses were divided into sub-groups depending on their eventual use. The standard MB came in two versions, one with a 45-seat front entrance, centre exit body, and the other with a 50-seat front entrance/exit layout.

The MBs were for use on conventional services converted to driver-only. The other two classes, coded MBA and MBS, had front entrance, centre exit bodies with room for 25 seated passengers and standing area for 48. The MBAs were designed for Red Arrow work and were fitted with slot machines and turnstiles. The MBSs were intended for London Transport's new central area suburban flat fare 'standee' services and the 'Autofare' routes in the country area which were to operate with graduated fares. They were all fitted with automatic fare collection machines so passengers could serve themselves. LT was anxious to tailor its new buses to the task they were expected to perform and was determined that the new style services were not going to cause more problems then they solved.

But things did not go as smoothly as planned. Protracted negotiations with the Trade Unions over the introduction of driver-only buses caused the postponement of the first 'area' schemes planned for introduction in April 1968. It was not until July that both sides reached agreement and on 7th September Bus Reshaping finally got under way with the introduction of new service pattern networks in Walthamstow and Wood Green. In the months that followed similar 'area' schemes, involving the introduction of single deckers on new flat-fare services as well as on graduated fare routes, began in Ealing, Stratford and Peckham, among others, with routes elsewhere being converted piecemeal.

Far from solving problems the new buses actually added to them. The popularity of the Red Arrows was not shared by their suburban counterparts. Despite an intensive publicity campaign there were delays at stops while passengers fumbled for the right money and the serve yourself ticket machines were unreliable. Having got past all that, many weary passengers could not find a vacant seat. All this made the new-style services slow and unpopular. Moreover the Merlins did not prove sufficiently robust for the work they had to do in London and their 36ft length caused problems in narrow and congested streets which had presented no difficulty to the shorter RT/RM buses they replaced. For its next large bus order London Transport opted for the shorter (33ft 5ins) AEC Swift, 838 of which were eventually acquired. As with the MBs there were sub-divisions of Swifts. The SM class were front entrance/exit 42-seater buses for the central bus area, while the bulk of the class (coded SMS) had front entrances and centre exits and could carry 67 passengers (33 seated and 34 standing). The body building for the SM family was shared by Marshalls of Cambridge, Metro-Cammell and Park Royal. All had AEC 505 132bhp engines.

The Swifts suffered from the same problems as the Merlins. Breakdowns were frequent, and spares became difficult to obtain as a result of materials shortages and labour troubles in the manufacturing industries. Moreover, the root cause of the whole exercise, staff shortage, was still affecting service reliability, while mechanical problems were making the driver-only routes unreliable too. It was a bleak time for London Transport, and rather a sad note on which to end its long, happy and eventful association with AEC, which finished with the delivery of the last SMS in March 1972. By this time AEC was part of British Leyland, which proceeded gradually to phase out the use of the AEC marque. On 25th May 1979 Leyland finally shut down the AEC factory at Southall where countless chassis for London buses had been built, thereby closing one of the most significant chapters in London bus history.

In the same year that the RCLs entered service, 14 of these Willowbrook-bodied AEC Reliances were purchased. Ideal for conversion to one-man operation, which later in life occurred, they were fitted with underfloor engines and were painted in a unique livery. RC 5 is seen at Victoria. Capital Transport

On a dull and wet morning in April 1966 London Transport's first high-capacity one-man operated buses entered service. These gave Londoners their first taste of 'standee' single deckers; the accommodation being for 25 seated and 49 standing passengers. Capital Transport

In 1968 a start was made on the introduction of high-capacity omo buses in the suburbs. In common with the Red Arrow vehicles, these incorporated self-service turnstiles for the payment of the flat-fare; these were later removed because of problems with reliability. To help familiarise passengers with the new vehicles, buses were put on display at important locations prior to their entry into service. MBS 473 is seen at Lower Edmonton terminus. Capital Transport

All the routes on London Transport's new flat-fare networks had a letter code as part of the route number, S for Stratford, P for Peckham and so on. The first schemes centred on Walthamstow and Wood Green and the letter W was used for both. MBS 208 is seen here on Walthamstow's route W21. Capital Transport

Shorter versions (33ft 5ins) of the original high-capacity single deckers entered service in 1970 following problems with the 36ft buses. During the seventies, these 'Swifts' were a common sight all over suburban London. SMS 86 is seen working from Edgware garage. Capital Transport

Another 'first', and a very significant one for London's bus passengers, was the introduction of London Transport's first driver-only double-deck bus route, the 233, in November 1969. E. Shirras

UPSTAIRS REGAINED

In 1967 restrictions on the operation of driver-only double-deck buses had been lifted. This came too late for London Transport which, in any case, had outstanding orders for several hundred single deckers, each with carrying capacities equal to or in excess of its RT and RM buses.

However, in November 1969, route 233 (West Croydon — Roundshaw) was converted from one-man RF to one-man XA. The 233 schedule required only one bus, but this conversion provides another entry for our extensive log of London bus 'firsts' because the 233 was the first London route to be operated by a driver-only double decker. The XAs were used on a new Croydon flat-fare network the following April, by which time LT had ordered 17 Daimler Feetlines with Park Royal bodies for delivery later in the year. Before the first one arrived the order had been increased by a further 100, London Transport nailing its colours in support of the double decker firmly to the mast.

The first of the new Fleetlines were exhibited at the 1970 Commercial Motor Show. London Transport had decided to give its new bus a name, 'The Londoner', a rather misplaced epithet since the vehicle was essentially of a provincial pedigree with minor London styling. The 'Londoner' tag was soon dropped, and from its debut on routes 95 and 220 on 2nd January 1971 the DMS gradually became a familiar sight all over London, not just on the RT/RM routes it converted to opo, but also on the capacity-strained single-deck services which it converted back to double-deck.

The Fleetlines were powered by Gardner 6LXB 10.45-litre engines, and the body building for the class was shared by Park Royal and Metro-Cammell. With new 89-passenger DMSs being used to replaced the unreliable MB/SM buses, the opo conversion programme slowed down. A batch of Fleetlines was built especially for crew operation and enabled withdrawal of RTs without increasing overall the level of driver-only operation in the fleet. The Merlins and Swifts were sold, mostly for scrap, many being broken up alongside life-expired RTs 20 years their senior.

A view which sums up the seventies for London's bus travellers — driver-only buses right in the heart of the City. In 1988 route 95 has the distinction of having been operated by Daimler Fleetlines for longer than any other route in the capital; this photo was taken when the DMSs first entered service in January 1971. Capital Transport

The last batch of DMSs delivered in 1976/77 were designed to be quieter than the rest of the class and had a modified engine shroud. These were known as the B20 DMSs. Most of the earlier members of the class were sold in the early 1980s, many for service elsewhere. Some even returned to London bus routes sporting the liveries of other operators working routes under contract for London Transport. The last DMSs in regular London Buses service were withdrawn at the end of 1992.

LONDON'S BUSES IN THE SEVENTIES AND EIGHTIES

London's bus engineers have always been anxious to test new vehicle concepts as they were developed, and the Experimental shop at Chiswick Works often concealed a new chassis or even a complete bus acquired for close examination. Sometimes the vehicles actually found their way into passenger service so they could be tested under 'field' conditions. No longer producing its own buses, despite an abortive attempt at a new design in the mid-1970s, LT had to know the potential of the buses which were available in an ever-developing market.

When the order for Swifts was completed 12 new single deckers of two new designs were purchased, six Metro-Scanias and six Leyland Nationals, an example of the former having been tried out in 1970 and the latter being Leyland's newly-developed and appropriately named standard single decker which, by 1973 when the LT order was delivered, was becoming a common sight nationwide. London Transport had ordered the 10-metre version of the National and, apart from the standard LT seat moquette and the familiar red livery, there was little to distinguish the six from the hundreds of others running up and down the country. By 1981 Leyland Nationals had replaced all the remaining Merlins and Swifts on the routes which London Transport had decided would remain single-deck, and the Mark II version had exclusive control of the Red Arrow network. Like the RMLs, many Mark II Nationals have undergone something of a transformation, being modernised with completely new body styling under the National Greenway project.

One of the six Anglo-Swedish Metro-Scania single deckers purchased by London Transport in 1973 is seen here on route S2, which was also used to test six Leyland Nationals during the same period. Barry Le Jeune

Following the trial of the Metro-Scania single deckers, London Transport purchased 164 of the double-deck version. These buses, named Metropolitans, entered service on central London trunk routes in 1976. They later moved to one-man work in south east London. MD 11 is seen in the Edgware Road near Marble Arch. Capital Transport

In the autumn of 1972 at the request of the GLC, London Transport introduced four experimental minibus services in areas and along roads where demand did not justify running full-size buses. The buses used were 16-seat Ford Transits, and one is seen here on route W9 leaving Highlands Hospital near Winchmore Hill on the first day of minibus operation in October 1972.
Capital Transport

Leyland Nationals started to arrive with London Transport in quantity in the mid-seventies, a total of 500 being purchased following the initial trial batch of half a dozen. Most are still providing service today. LS 330 is seen at Harrow in 1980.
Capital Transport

Bristol LH single deckers were purchased for routes unsuitable for larger vehicles. Route 247, on which BL 11 is seen, had a width restriction at Warley.
Capital Transport

As RF replacement drew near, 95 Bristol LH6L single deckers powered by Leyland 125bhp engines with 39-seat Eastern Coach Works bodies were purchased for the routes where the operation of the larger Leyland Nationals might have caused problems. The BLs were only 7ft 6ins wide, the narrowest London buses since the RT. There were also 17 of a shorter version, coded BS, which LT found useful on some routes originally introduced with minibuses.

The Scania single deckers, coded MS, did not enjoy long service with London Transport and most had been disposed of by 1978. But they did play a part in subsequent developments. In 1973 Metro-Cammell produced a prototype double-deck version of the Scania, the 'Metropolitan'. The unusual dual-length front windscreen layout, which originated with the single-deck version, was perpetuated with the Metropolitan, which otherwise bore a strong resemblance to the DMS. London Transport engineers inspected the prototype and in 1974 placed an order for 164 vehicles, classified MD, which entered service at Peckham and New Cross garages between March 1976 and February 1977. The MDs sported a new livery of red with white relief around the upper deck windows and it was soon applied to new DMSs as well, making a pleasant change from the predominantly red schemes used on London buses since 1950. The MDs were crew operated and in this form carried 72 passengers (29 on the lower deck and 43 upstairs), but like the single-deck Scanias they were destined for a short life in London. Being a small class by comparison with others in the fleet, the decision was taken to dispose of them when some 600 buses were rendered surplus by service cuts introduced following the Law Lords ruling over cheap fares in 1982.

The MDs ended their days in 1984 as one-person operated buses in south-east London, but their place in the capital's bus history is secure because in 1977 Metro-Cammell took the Metropolitan concept to its next stage and produced an all-British version which it named 'Metrobus'. LT ordered five Metrobuses as an initial batch, the first, coded MT 1, being delivered in April 1978. M 5 (the code was changed with the delivery of M 4), was the last London bus to be built with a three-box route display. The production batch, delivery of which began in February 1979, had a single aperture two-piece display, the route number and the via points being on the same blind with the ultimate destination displayed below.

The London Metrobus is the standard MCW product. It seats 71 (43 upstairs and 28 down). In January 1988 there were 1,426 Mark I Metrobuses in the London Buses fleet. They are powered by Gardner 6LXB 10.45-litre 160bhp engines, a far cry from the 28hp engine of the B-type.

The three principal double-deck types on London's red bus services today are the Metrobus, the Titan and the trusty Routemaster. This view shows Metrobus M 10 and RM 289 at Fulwell in 1981. Routemasters have since disappeared from suburban services such as the 281, those remaining being concentrated on central London trunk routes.
John Reed

Park Royal Vehicles, builders of countless London bus bodies, closed down after the delivery of the last of the initial batch of Titans in 1980. From this batch, T 28 is seen on the outskirts of Romford in 1980 on a route today operated by Capital Citybus under contract to LRT. Capital Transport

Meanwhile Leyland, in consultation with London Transport, had developed a bus especially suited to London conditions but with a market potential elsewhere. Leyland called the project B15 and the designers resurrected some of the features of the FRM. A plywood mock-up was constructed in 1973 and a small batch of prototypes was built and made available for trial in 1975. LT tested two of the prototypes, which were given the name 'Titan', between 1975 and 1978, using them on crew-operated route 24 (Hampstead Heath — Pimlico) before placing an order for 250.

The first production Titans (T class) were delivered in August 1978 and, following the customary period of staff familiarisation and training, they entered service the following December on routes from Hornchurch garage, just as the first single deckers bearing the same famous class code had done exactly 49 years earlier.

The Titans, with their 66-seat (22 downstairs, 44 up) Park Royal bodies powered by Gardner 6LXB engines, were delivered at the same time as the Metrobuses although each type was confined to separate operating divisions.

Unhappily the Titan was dogged by the bad fortune which had been hovering around London's buses for many years. Production was hardly under way when Leyland announced that it was shutting down the Park Royal factory in west London. The factory had been building London bus bodies since the thirties and it finally closed in 1981 after the initial order for 250 Ts had been completed. Leyland transferred Titan production to its Workington plant, but the move north caused a lengthy interruption to deliveries. By December 1981 there were only 370 Ts in the fleet, against 700 Metrobuses. Although the Titan was proving reliable in London service, Leyland were disappointed with orders from elsewhere, an important factor if the bus was to remain in production. Some were built for Greater Manchester and Reading Corporation, but this was not enough for Leyland and the company announced in 1983 that Titan production was to cease, which it did following the delivery of T 1125 in November 1984. At about the same time MCW introduced a Mark II version of the Metrobus and began to phase out production of the Mark I type, which ceased on completion of the LT order with M 1440 in January 1986. It was time for LT to go to market again.

One of the three Dennis Dominators purchased by LT in 1984 is seen working from Brixton garage following its transfer there from Stockwell, which was used on the base for the bus comparison trials. The three vehicles of this batch are now owned by Capital Citybus. John Miller

The Olympian also featured in the 1984 trials, three being purchased with ECW bodywork. Northern Counties bodied Olympians were bought for the setting up of the short-lived Bexleybus operation in south east London in 1987. Mike Harris

Whether there will be any scope for a centralised bus designing function with London Buses split into separate units with privatisation in mind is somewhat doubtful. Work had started on the next generation of London bus, incorporating features such as lower step heights and brighter interior decor. The bright green handrails, designed to assist partially-sighted passengers, were adopted for the Olympians and MkII Metrobuses delivered to London Buses in 1986/87. London Buses Ltd

LAST ORDERS

One of the purposes of this book is to illustrate various contrasts between London's buses of today and yesterday. If we apply that criterion here we can do no better than to contrast 1984 with 1904, the year the LGOC ordered a variety of different bus chassis to test before placing a quantity order. In 1984 London Transport/LRT took delivery of a small number of new buses for precisely the same purpose. The order comprised of three Leyland Olympians, three Mark II Metrobuses, three Volvo Ailsas, and three Dennis Dominators.

The first to arrive in February 1984 was a Leyland Olympian, the bus designed as the replacement for the Bristol VRT, the standard National Bus Company double decker. At a glance the Olympian strongly resembles the Titan but there are many differences, one being that the Olympian (L class) is two inches shorter in height at 14ft 2½ins. Olympians seat 75 passengers (28 downstairs and 47 up) as against the 66-seater Titans, but they have in common the fact that they are powered by the Gardner 6LXB engine. They formed the only bulk order placed as a direct result of the trials and after the establishment of LRT in June 1984.

The Metrobuses, Volvos and Dennises were put through their paces, along with the Olympians, on opo routes from Stockwell garage in 1984/85. Probably the most interesting vehicles, from the point of view of innovation, were the Volvos because these had front-mounted engines. Indeed one of the Volvos (V 3) actually had a rear platform, the first new London bus to have one since 1968, though it had a front entrance as well. V 3 ran on crew operated routes, like the 77, before being modified in 1986 to conform with the others which were built to the standard opo layout.

The Mark II Metrobuses were merely a progression of the earlier version but built using a simpler construction method. The Dennises, with their Northern Counties bodies, were the first from this manufacturer to operate in London since 1937.

DECLINE OF THE DOUBLE-DECKER

In the years since 1987 far fewer new double deckers have been delivered for service in London than at any time since 1970; just 198 of the larger 'big buses' as they are now known, in service at the end of 1993 were delivered since L 263, the last of the main batch of Leyland Olympians, arrived in January 1987. The Olympian fleet was increased by the addition of 23 (L 292-314) Leyland bodied examples early in 1990 for RiversideBus route 237, and a further 40 with Alexander dual-door bodies (L 315-364) in the spring of 1992 to work on routes from Stamford Hill garage.

But what of L 264-291? These buses were leased to work on routes in the Bexleybus network. They had Northern Counties bodies and were clad in the Bexleybus blue and cream livery. They ran from the inception of Bexleybus in 1988 until the operation came to an end early in 1991 after which they left London for other parts of the country.

On a more stable front, LBL subsidiary London General acquired 39 Northern Counties bodied Volvo Citybuses with Volvo TDH101GB 11-litre engines in 1989/90. Numbered VC 1-39, the entire class works from Stockwell garage.

Scania is another bus builder to supply vehicles for London service since 1989, 71 of them in fact, bodied by either Alexander (S 1-29) or Northern Counties (S 30-71). All are powered by Scania's DS11-25 11-litre engine. They work on routes operated by LBL subsidiaries London Northern and East London, the latter using several in special livery on its Docklands Express network.

Latest in the ever dwindling world of the double-decker is the Optare Spectra. Looking every inch (or centimetre) buses for the 1990s, these handsome vehicles, coded SP are powered by DAF RS200 8.65-litre engines and work from London Central's Brixton garage, usually on route 3.

The double-deck bus has a future in London, but whether it's a future which extends very far into the outer suburbs seems at present doubtful.

REVIVAL OF THE SINGLE DECKER

Single-deck fortunes have revived. After LT's rather unhappy flirtation with large capacity single-deckers on busy routes in the late 60s and early 70s the association has resumed. In 1989 the LBL units were given powers to order new buses providing their submissions were sanctioned by the Company's financial management. Several unique vehicles were obtained for evaluation in the early 1990s prior to orders being placed, including two Renault PR1002s, both with 51-seater Northern Counties bodies, one of which was purchased and coded RN1. Others included a DAF Bendibus loaned from South Yorkshire Transport, and a couple of Optare/DAF Deltas, an evaluation which resulted in orders eventually totalling 53. The Delta (class DA) is the single-deck counterpart to the Spectra, and is powered by DAF's LC1160 11.6-litre engine. Ten are with subsidiary Westlink with the remainder at East London's Barking garage. The latter are in a very attractive silver livery which has not been perpetuated on subsequent single-deckers like the LA, LN and VN classes which made their debut on busy central London routes in 1992/93.

The LAs are 16 Alexander bodied Dennis Lances with Cummins 6CT8 engines. They seat 39 passengers and at the time of writing operate from Catford garage on route 36B. Their use on such a busy service has not been without controversy, and during 1994 the 36B is expected to regain double-deckers. Similar chassis and engines to those on the LAs power the 31 LNs; the only difference is the 37-seater Northern Counties bodywork. The LNs arrived in 1993 and are based with Metroline. Volvo units provide the base for the 13 members of the VN class. These buses, used exclusively on route 88, have 40-seater Northern Counties bodies.

Entering service in 1994 is a large batch of low floor single-deckers designed specifically to cater for disabled passengers. The order comprises 30 Scanias and 38 Dennis Lances, all having bodywork by Wrights of Ballymena.

London Buses' first sizeable orders for large single-deckers since the early 1980s went to DAF/Optare for their new Delta, 35 of which were delivered between 1989 and 1993. LBL subsidiary East London have 25, which are all based at Barking garage. Martin Ruthe

Some controversy has surrounded the replacement of double-deckers by large single-deckers on some routes, but the policy continues in 1994. An early example was the allocation of 39-seater Dennis Lances on route 36B in 1992. Martin Ruthe

Route 88 fell to the single-decker in the spring of 1993. The new order, branded *The Clapham Omnibus*, comprises the entire **VN** class. **VN 4** is seen in Great Smith Street, Westminster. R.J. Waterhouse

THE MIDIBUS REVOLUTION

The route restructuring and local networking which has been a prominent feature of LRT's competitive tendering process has brought a host of new faces to the London bus scene. These are the midi and mini-buses which have become a familiar sight not just around London, but right in the centre as well. At the start of 1994 there were over 1,400 of them in service with London Buses, a stark contrast to the beginning of 1988 when there were fewer than 50. This small number included the remnants of the Ford Transit based FS class, which London Transport had used in its 1972 minibus experiments, and two Dodge 50s from 1982 built for use on Potters Bar local route PB1.

But since the Orpington scheme in 1986 until the present, the 'small' bus has been seen in ever increasing numbers; so much so that at the end of 1993 there were 19 separate classes of midi and minibus, although only five manufacturers have been involved in building chassis for them. The main supplier is Dennis Vehicles, which has provided over 650 of its Dart chassis in both 8.5 and 9 metre versions. Other well known makers include Mercedes-Benz, Renault, Fiat and Metro-Cammell. Bodywork comes from a variety of sources, as the list below will illustrate.

Briefly the midi and minibus classes are composed thus:

DENNIS
DR/DRL (Total 313 at end 1993) Reeve Burgess bodywork (DR1-19), Plaxton Pointer bodies on
    remainder (1990 onwards)
DT (Total 168) Duple bodywork (DT1-27 and 168), Carlyle bodies on remainder (1990/91)
DW/DWL (Total 196) Wright bodywork. (1990 onwards)

All London Buses' Dennis Darts are powered by Cummins 6BT5 engines.

MERCEDES-BENZ
MA (Total 134) Alexander bodywork (1988/91)
MC (Total 5) Carlyle bodywork (1989/90)
MT/MTL (Total 14) Reeve Burgess bodywork (1988/91)
MW (Total 37) Wright bodywork (1989/93)
SR (Total 123) Optare bodywork (1988/89)
    Most are based on the Mercedes-Benz 811D chassis; the exception is the MT class which has the 709D version. Power comes from the Mercedes DM364A 3.64 engine.

OPTARE/METRO-CAMMELL
OV (Total 24) Optare City Pacer bodies on Volkswagen LT55 chassis powered by VW 2.4-litre engines.
    These vehicles, only the first five of which bore the class identification OV pioneered the late 1980s minibus revival in London. The unnumbered ones were used by LRT on route C1 which served previously busless areas of Kensington and Westminster. All had been withdrawn by the end of 1991.
MR/MRL (Total 241) Originally marketed as the Metrorider by Metro-Cammell, which built both bodies and chassis. Optare took over production when MCW closed down in 1991, building MRL 135 onwards. The Cummins 6B engine provides the motive power.

FIAT
FM (Total 10) Marshall bodywork (1993)
FR (Total 8) Reeve Burgess bodywork (1990)
RH (Total 24) These 21-seater Robin Hood bodied minibuses launched, with the OVs, London's first minibus network, 'Roundabout', in the Orpington area in 1986. By 1993 only four survived. All the Fiat based minibuses are fitted with Iveco 8140 series 2.5-litre engines.

RENAULT
RB (Total 33) Renault 50 chassis, Reeve Burgess bodywork (1989/90)
RW (Total 90) Renault 75 chassis, Wright bodywork (1990)
The Renault minis are all powered by Perkins Phaser 110T 3.99-litre engines.

CITY VEHICLE ENGINEERING
CV (Total 7) CVE built both chassis and bodies for the 20-seater CVs which are fitted with 2.5-litre Land Rover engines.

A sparsely filled StarRider (SR 74) works a journey on route 396 at Bromley in August 1993. Martin Ruthe

Carlyle bodied Dennis Dart, DT 61, works a Sunday journey on the 9, a busy central London route long associated with heavily loaded, crew double-deckers. Such a sight is a 1990s phenomenon likely to spill over into the next century, especially as routes like the 11 and 74 now have midibus offshoots running in the central area all week. Martin Ruthe

Probably the best looking of the new generation of small London bus is the Wright bodied Dennis Dart. Perhaps the slight resemblance to the much loved RF class has something to do with it. At Wimbledon in November 1992 we find London General *Streetline* DW 129 working a duty on former 'big bus' route 155. Martin Ruthe

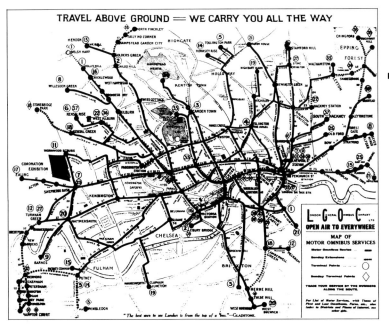

LGOC Map, 1911

"The best way to see London is from the top of a 'bus."—GLADSTONE.

Chapter 3
PROVIDING THE SERVICE

Everything connected with London bus travel has developed, or altered in some way, since the earliest days of the horse bus. If you think about it a bus journey is made up of several component parts. Probably the best way to see how each has changed is to take an imaginary bus journey — spanning nearly 160 years.

PUBLICITY
Before the journey starts we must decide the best route to our destination. Easily obtainable bus route information, in the form of maps and timetables, is as important to the bus operator as it is to the traveller, and London's bus passengers are fortunate in that good publicity has been a feature of the capital's buses for many years.

The illustrated Omnibus Guide, first published in May 1851, is an early example. It cost 6d (2½p) and was probably a best seller in the year of the Great Exhibition in Hyde Park for the Omnibus proprietors did excellent business. The Guide listed over 150 different services and gave details of the routes travelled, including the places of interest passed en route, times and frequencies as well as fares. Many entries featured drawings of the bus sides showing the proprietors' emblems, so that potential passengers could recognise particular coaches. Most of the emblems were merely the names of the areas served, like BRENTFORD, WESTMINSTER, or BOW & STRATFORD, but some have a more charismatic air, TAGLIONI, PARAGON, BRITISH QUEEN and even ENTRANTRESS. Others bore names of the Association to which the bus proprietor belonged such as HOLBORN, BANK & OXFORD STREET CONVEYANCE SOCIETY and CAMBERWELL & DULWICH CONVEYANCE ASSOCIATION. Despite the mixed fortunes of the omnibus proprietors after 1851 some form of route and company information was still published, one of the more notable publications being Mogg's Omnibus and Cab Guide published during the latter part of the nineteenth century. But route publicity direct from individual operators was so sparse as to be almost non-existent. Even the LGOC does not seem to have produced much route information before the summer of 1910, by which time it had adopted Vanguard's route numbering system and was building a dependable motor bus — its B-type. So with services becoming more reliable and the routes easier to follow what better way to publicise its services than by giving away free maps with all its routes listed? From 1911 the General was producing maps of its services at regular intervals, usually monthly, although during the First World War and in the years immediately following, the number of issues was reduced to just a handful each year. By the 'twenties the monthly issue pattern had been re-established with maps and leaflets listing the routes being obtainable simply by asking the bus conductor, who was also expected to be conversant with the times of the first and last journeys on his route. Some of the publications were quite ambitious with drawings, or even photographs, being included, and several listed the routes which the General ran in association with other operators in the Home Counties. Fares, running times and 'via' points were also included. The LGOC produced some Green Line publicity in 1932/33 which took the form of guides with maps.

Map issues continued at monthly intervals until the formation of the LPTB in 1933 when the rate of issue was reduced to four or five each year.

LT produced separate maps for its central bus, Green Line and Tram/Trolleybus services, as well as the Underground, but for some reason a separate map of its extensive country bus network did not appear until 1948.

Since 1970 only two or three red bus maps have been issued each year and the more recent 'London Wide' issues have included other operators' local services (including those provided under contract to LRT) as well as those run by London Buses. The bus map is still one of the most popular items of publicity material produced at 55 Broadway. Since 1980 some area bus route maps have been produced and distributed free to homes in those areas.

But a map can only help with route planning, not timing. This is why for many years after its formation, in fact right up until 1969, London Transport published area timetable books, in some form or other, to cover most of its route territory.

The Inspectors' famous 'Red' bus timetable book was also available in public form for many years. It contained detailed information and timetables for most of London's 300 red bus routes and first and last journey times for the more frequent services. Similar books, in area format, were available for London Transport's Country Area until 1969 and London Country carried these on for several years after its formation in 1970.

As well as the maps countless leaflets and handbills have been produced over the years giving information on bus route amendments, the introduction of new facilities and details of holiday services.

For most of the 1970s little or no timetable information, at least in booklet form, was produced, but in 1982 free area timetable booklets were reintroduced on a small scale. By 1986 thirty-one issues were available covering the whole of Greater London and all were being distributed house-to-house. These were superseded in 1987 by a series of 33 Local Bus Guides, leaflets giving service and route frequency information which are complemented by regular 'Updates'.

The local guides survive today, but are now regarded as part of the all-embracing London Bus Information System. The System, developed in 1993 by Fitch Consultancy, is designed to simplify the way information is presented to bus users. The process includes bus stop information as well as the local bus guides. Fitch has also been contracted to produce the all-system bus map. Other bus service information publicity, including booklets giving details of route changes, is produced both in-house and by outside agencies.

THE BUS STOP

Having decided on the route to take our travellers now go to the nearest stop to wait for their bus: but it wasn't always like this. Although buses ran on fixed routes, before the 1930s passengers could hail a bus wherever it suited them, and buses could stop anywhere, within reason, to pick up passengers or set them down. Convenient, but it could play havoc with bus running times, and as London's traffic increased so the problem became worse. In 1913 the LGOC experimented with a few fixed stops, but it wasn't until the 1920s that the Company introduced bus stops at the busiest places and actively encouraged passengers to use them. Even so, buses still had to stop when required, official stop or not.

The LPTB soon grasped the nettle and began to increase the number of fixed stops, recognising that the stop-anywhere principle was contributing to service delays. It urged its customers to use the stops and in March 1935 introduced an experimental scheme whereby stops were placed along an entire stretch of route from Euston Road to Tottenham. The stops were either compulsory, where buses had to stop, or request, where passengers could either hail the bus they wanted to board or ring the bell once if they wished to alight. By 1937 nearly 150 miles of road had fixed stops and LT continued the strategy, either by fitting stops along

Original LGOC style	1921	1934

specified routes or in designated areas. By the early post-war period the whole of LT's vast area had fixed bus stops. The stops, and the posts supporting them, have altered over the years: the photographs show just how. In the 1930s both concrete and cast iron posts were used. The latter, known as Birmingham Guild posts, were always employed where an inspector's telephone had to be fixed to the stop so that the wiring could be channelled down their hollow centres. By the outbreak of war in 1939 a more stylish terrazzo post had been designed, incorporating either one or two timetable frames. The basic design has remained unchanged to this day. The modern stop flags are especially shaped to be weather resistant. A recent idea, at busier places at least, is to put the location on the stop flag. The familiar bullseye-flagged stop, atop its concrete post, was the one piece of street furniture which more than anything else created a huge new 'London', far beyond the statutory 'Londons' created by parliament, the post office or the police, for whenever you saw a London Transport bus stop, whether in Gravesend, Greenwich, Harrow or Hitchin, you were in London, the London of public transport. After the formation of London Country in 1970 the bullseye stops were gradually replaced outside the 'red bus' area by those favoured by the Department of Transport and 'London' retracted into its boundaries once more.

1939	1952	1988

The LPTB had the provision of shelters for bus passengers as a high priority and the early ones were very handsome affairs. The photographer of this one in Fencepiece Road, Barkingside provides a welcome diversion for the damp humanity sheltering from the rain awaiting the departure of the route 25A bus in December 1935. LT Museum 23264

SHELTERS

Shelters for bus passengers were few and far between in the early days, indeed most of the shelters in London were provided by the LCC Tramways Department for its more fortunate customers. The LPTB wasted little time in designing and installing modern shelters with seating and good provision for route maps and publicity. In fact the first shelters erected in 1934/5 acted as a focal point for passengers to wait for buses, even before fixed stops were installed. They were stylish flat-roofed metal and glass affairs, and some of the early ones boasted one, or even two, large LT bullseyes on their roofs. During the war something a little less lavish was produced; this was the aluminium framed 'Q' shelter, which was little more than a free-standing frame bolted to the pavement. The 'Q' shelter, much beloved by children who happily spent the moments before their bus arrived by somersaulting over the cross bars was, in a modified form, produced until the 1960s. By this time some areas, especially the more exposed places, had been graced with handsome enclosed wooden structures like the 'Keston' designed by London Transport and named after the location of the first one to be installed. LT also purchased the wooden Astolet shelter recognisable by its pointed roof. Both types, unlike the very basic and exposed aluminium framed shelter, had seating. A number of cantilever concrete shelters were also acquired but these proved unsatisfactory.

In the late-1980s, it is still possible to stand out of the rain under a 'Keston', an Astolet or a 'Q', but the majority of today's shelters comprise either enclosed or cantilever Abacus models — designed by LT and installed throughout the seventies — or Adshels, with their advertisement panels providing a useful source of revenue. Adshel is in partnership with LRT and produces the bulk of advertising shelters, although other makes are used on occasions. Tip-up seats have been fitted in most shelters since 1983. At present there are some 8,000 bus shelters in LRT's area, over 3,000 of them advertising shelters. Many stops, particularly on busy highways, are now situated in pull-in bays to avoid delaying fast traffic flows. A system of bus stop clearways, marked by double yellow lines and blips, has been in operation since 1971.

The 'Q' shelter, a rather spartan affair introduced during the war, became common in the forties and fifties and a few examples can still be seen today.
Capital Transport

London Transport Advertising and the advertising shelter firm Adshel have joined forces in London to bring commercial advertising to bus shelters. An early version is shown publicising Adshel's own product, while a later design is seen flanked by a disused bus stop and a temporary 'dolly' stop. The bus stop is probably being moved further forward in this mid-seventies view due to the onward march of the front-entrance bus.
Capital Transport

UPTON PARK (BOLEYN)
HIGH ST NORTH
PLASHET GROVE
GREEN STREET

UPTON PARK (BOLEYN)
VIA
BARKING ROAD

BARKING BY PASS HIGH ST SOUTH
GREEN STREET
BARKING ROAD
HIGH ST SOUTH

DAGENHAM FORD WORKS
MANOR WAY
BARKING BY PASS RIPPLE RD
NEW RD KENT AVENUE

NTH WOOLWICH FREE FERRY
KENT AVENUE NEW RD
RIPPLE RD BARKING BY PASS
MANOR WAY

UPTON PARK REDCLYFFE ROAD
HIGH ST SOUTH
BARKING ROAD
GREEN STREET

EPPING FOREST WARREN WOOD HOUSE
HIGH ST EAST HAM ALDERSBROOK RD
HIGH ST WANSTEAD EAGLE LA
WOODFORD RD EPPING NEW RD

NTH WOOLWICH FREE FERRY
EPPING NEW RD WOODFORD RD
EAGLE LANE HIGH ST WANSTEAD
ALDERSBROOK RD HIGH ST EAST HAM

PRIVATE
To HIRE A BUS
APPLY:- 55 BROADWAY. S.W.I.

This photograph of the blind making shop at Chiswick
Works was taken in 1935 when both roller blinds and a
few of the old style destination boards were being
made. The boards were for the NS class, the last London
double deckers to have them. LT Museum U19556

BLINDS

If Londoners fail to appreciate the aesthetic qualities of their buses there is at least one feature which they eagerly look for, the route information blind. Close study of the photographs in this book will reveal the many and varied ways in which route information has been displayed on buses since the early days and those with experience of other bus operators at home or abroad will readily acknowledge how full and detailed London bus route displays are by comparison. Like everything else in our story route information on buses has developed along with the vehicles themselves. Horse bus passengers soon associated the colour of the local omnibuses with the Associations which operated them and the routes they worked. In most cases details of the route were painted along the vehicle sides as the route was rarely altered. In later years horse buses were fitted with moveable destination boards which were usually positioned above or below the side windows. Some even displayed route numbers in their final days.

The motor age with its quicker speeds and new companies, with new liveries and routes, required something different and the information was more conspicuously displayed. The best location for route information was at the front above the driver's position so that passengers could see it in advance of the bus stopping. The LGOC, and most of the other companies, displayed the route number and destination information in black lettering on a white background slipboard. The destination boards could be reversed at each end of the route, a system the pirates found useful with its opportunity to switch course in mid-route and cream off traffic along a more profitable thoroughfare.

The boards were to remain a feature of London's buses right up until the introduction of the new AEC models (T, LT, ST) in 1929. These handsome vehicles were the first GENERAL buses to be fitted with roller destination blinds. Individual sections of a complete blind were composed using letters positioned on strips of white paper. A 'screen' of silk was then placed on top of the sheet which was then inked in black, or any desired colour, using a blade which drew the ink across the silk screen. When all the individual displays had dried they were laid in correct sequence on a board and then gummed onto a roll of cotton cut to the required length, up to a maximum of about 36ft. Today, all new blinds for London buses are produced by an outside contractor and printed directly onto rolls of strong paper, enabling blind lengths of 60ft or more. The last blinds produced by the traditional method were supplied to Victoria garage in August 1988.

TICKETS AND TICKET MACHINES

The issue of bus tickets is a commonplace feature of bus travel, yet surprisingly for many years bus passengers were not issued with tickets as receipts for fares paid at all. Traditionally coach operators had written out tickets for their passengers but the short distances and constant coming and going of omnibus travel did not make practical such a laborious task. So London's first bus passengers just paid their fares to the conductor as they left the bus, not knowing whether their copper coins would ever reach the bus company coffers. It was generally recognised that conductors kept back some of the takings to share with drivers and horsekeepers.

Early in its existence the LGOC introduced the correspondence ticket transfer system similar to that operated in Paris. The tickets were valid on more than one bus and enabled a change to be made en route. There was not much demand for transfer tickets and none were issued after 1858, most bus journeys still being made without any form of receipt.

In an early attempt at fare checking, conductors marked on a form the number of passengers that had travelled on their buses during particular spells of duty. They then paid in a corresponding sum in takings. A regular check was made by plain clothes inspectors. The LGOC maintained its counting system for many years, seemingly in the full knowledge that it was being abused by staff, who had to be careful not to pay in too little in takings for fear of arousing suspicion. The practice, and the half hearted way the General tried to remedy it, was a source of annoyance to the company's shareholders, who no doubt took great interest in the ticket-issuing system introduced by London Roadcar when it started business in 1881. Roadcar used a system of numbered tickets which enabled a more accurate check to be kept on fares paid. Later the Bell Punch ticket machine was used by the company to

Left **The Bell Punch ticket machine, which validated thick paper tickets held in a rack until issue, was a common sight on London's road public transport for more than 60 years. It was superseded in the 1950s by the Gibson ticket machine, still in use on crew-operated services today.** Right **The first generation of self-service ticket machines as fitted to an SMS type vehicle in 1970.** LT Museum

validate tickets for specific journeys and by 1890 the Bell Punch system was being used by many bus and tram operators except the General and its associates. It seems that the General only took positive steps to adopt an all-ticket system after it had been approached with the idea of selling advertising space on the ticket backs. In 1891 the company decided to adopt the Bell Punch system, implementing it on 31st May after having first increased staff wages to avoid a dispute. This was to no avail because the General's crews did strike, from 6th June, bringing out the staff of most of the other bus companies, including Roadcar, in the process. The strike lasted a week and is noteworthy not just in that it ushered in an era of better staff conditions, but it was also one of the first strikes involving a Trade Union.

Very soon the conductors with their rack of Bell Punch tickets to hand and cancelling machines strapped to their tunics became a familiar sight on London's road transport and were to remain so for more than half a century. In the heyday of the Bell Punch, 4,000 million tickets were printed each year.

The Bell Punch survived several attempts to supersede it until 1953, when the Gibson ticket machine, designed by George Gibson, former Superintendent at London Transport's Effra Road ticket machine works, made its appearance.

The Gibson carried a single roll of paper on which could be printed a variety of different ticket denominations just by turning a wheel on the side of the machine to the appropriate fare. A built-in meter recorded the number and types of tickets issued. It took five years for the Bell Punch machines to be replaced, the last ones remaining in use at West Ham and Poplar trolleybus depots until October 1958.

The Gibson was not the only ticket machine to supersede the Bell Punch. Conductors on Green Line coaches used a machine called a Setright which was also based on the ticket roll principle.

When London Transport began converting some of its country area routes to driver-only operation in the fifties another new style of ticket machine was adopted. This was the Ultimate, a machine capable of issuing six different denominations of pre-printed ticket with considerable ease. Ultimates were also used on the central area RF buses on driver-only services from 1964.

In 1967 London Transport introduced another new machine, the Almex, which could be used by either conductors or driver/operators. The tickets issued from the Almex were smaller than those issued by the Gibson, so more tickets could be produced per roll. The Almex also made the job of totalling up the cash simpler by having a wider fare range so that conductors did not have to issue a combination of tickets for higher fare values as with the Gibson. The Almex contained a cassette which recorded up to 4,000 different fare transactions. It was thought that the information contained on the cassettes would be of value in collating information about passenger travel patterns.

The Almex became the standard ticket machine when opo was introduced on a large scale in the 1970s. Today's driver/operators also use a sophisticated computer-based machine called Wayfarer, perched on the corner of the cab area. The tickets issued by a Wayfarer give considerably more information than has previously been seen on bus tickets, including the date and time of issue, together with the garage code and running number of the bus involved.

On 22nd May 1983 London Transport unveiled the Travelcard, integrating bus and Underground fares on a zonal basis and available in a variety of forms. There are still zonal bus passes and there are also local Area Bus Passes available in fourteen suburban areas.

In October 1992 Wayfarer's new 'Clipper' electronic ticket machine was introduced on crew buses as a replacement for the Gibson. As an ominous sign of the times, the Clipper incorporates a personal alarm and, with the future very much in mind, can read Smartcards. Within the year Clippers had all but replaced the Gibson, the last examples of which were withdrawn from Westbourne Park garage in October 1993.

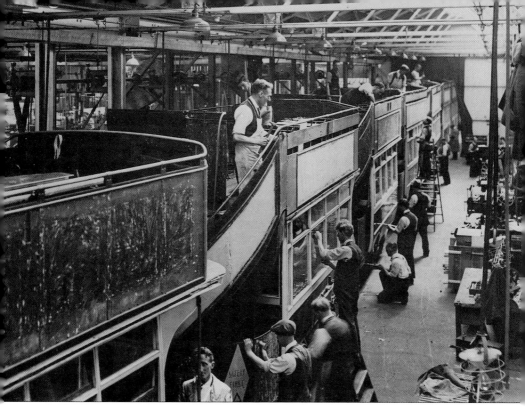

Overhauling and maintaining a bus fleet the size of London's has always been a labour-intensive business as this view of the Body Shop taken in the early days of Chiswick Works shows. The vehicles being worked on are K-types. LT Museum 22558

LOOKING AFTER THE FLEET

For London's buses, maintenance has for many years had two distinct levels, day-to-day care and the overhaul.

Buses usually come in two parts, the chassis, which includes the underframe, engine, gearbox, fuel tank, in fact the parts which make the bus go, and the body, the part which accommodates the passengers. Both parts need careful care and maintenance if they are to give their owner and the crews working on them trouble-free work and a long life.

This simple rule applies just as much to the 'high-tech' machines of the 1980s as it did to the horse bus, but in the earlier case care of the motive power source meant warmth, water and fodder.

The more buses a company owned the more practical it was to practise economies of scale, and the LGOC was an early exponent of this. It created central depots for horse feed distribution and vehicle overhaul and construction. By 1857 the General had opened its horse bus construction and overhaul works in North Road, Islington, and continued to use the establishment right up until plans had been drawn up for the building of Chiswick Works.

The arrival of the motor bus needed something a little more sophisticated than stables, many of which were adapted to take the new-fangled machines. But for the early motor bus mechanics, working conditions were primitive to say the least. Few garages had inspection pits, and what pits there were were rather insufficient for their purpose. After work, washing facilities for mechanics were sparse. But conditions gradually improved as new premises were built, and as bus designs became more complex so the methods used to maintain them evolved as well.

By the 1950s bus maintenance procedure in the garages had developed into one involving regular inspections on a three-week cycle. A bus would be cleaned each night, with any complaints or observations about its performance received from drivers or conductors who had worked on it during the day being looked into. Every third week an hour-long mechanical inspection would be carried out, and every nine weeks a more thorough 3½-hour examination would be made. Any defect found during these inspections would be rectified. Much longer inspections would be made at 18 and 36 week intervals.

The most extensive maintenance each bus received was an overhaul. The growth of services, and the rapid development of the motor bus, had made the General realise that the full centralisation of its bus overhaul activities was essential. Prior to the opening of Chiswick, the LGOC had maintained three bus overhaul works. In addition to North Road, overhaul work was also carried out at Seagrove Road, Fulham and Olaf Street, Hammersmith. The police required that every motor bus received a complete overhaul once a year, followed by an inspection, before it could re-enter service. In those days overhauling a bus was a rather time-consuming operation. Firstly a bus had to be taken from its garage to one of the overhaul works, where the body was removed. The chassis was then driven back to its home garage where the mechanical overhaul was carried out, and then returned to the works where body and chassis were reunited; the completed bus then returned to its garage. In 1921 the LGOC opened four central depots in preparation for the transfer of all bus overhaul work to Chiswick. These were located in existing garages, Hounslow, Dalston, Cricklewood and Willesden. Staff who had been involved in bus overhauling at the garages were transferred to one of the four depots to receive training before the final move to the giant new 31-acre bus construction, overhaul and development works at Chiswick. Work on it began in September 1920 and it was commissioned in May 1922.

The creation of a centralised works for bus overhaul enabled the General to save considerable sums in maintenance costs whilst setting standards in procedure which benefited its entire bus fleet. Further cost savings emerged from the development and introduction of oil engines in the early 1930s. When London Transport was created in 1933 all the buses it inherited from the independents went to Chiswick for repainting into the familiar red or country bus green liveries of London's new unified bus fleet. The requirement to give each bus an annual overhaul lasted until 1933 when control of passenger service vehicle operation passed to the Ministry of Transport, which required that bus operators were to keep vehicles in a safe and serviceable condition, and devised a system of inspections on the road, and in garages, to ensure that buses met the requirements. This change in the law enabled LT to plan its own overhaul cycle for its buses. By 1950 the interval between overhauls was 2½-3 years, depending on the type of bus. At that time replacement of London's remaining trams by diesel buses was under way, and between 1950 and 1953 London's bus fleet grew by 1,100 vehicles. Already Chiswick had ceased building new buses to concentrate on overhauling, but with a fleet of 7,000 vehicles requiring three-year overhauls it was realised that a larger works would be needed. In fact it was envisaged that by 1959 London Transport would be operating a fleet of 10,000 buses! This was never to be, but just the possibility of it was enough to sanction proposals for totally new facilities.

Some use as an overflow works was already being made of a site at Aldenham situated in green belt land by the Watford by-pass, which was to have been a large depot for the operation and maintenance of tube trains on an extension of the Northern Line from Edgware. Plans for this extension, held up by the war, were abandoned in the early 1950s.

LT decided to use the site as a major new works equipped to overhaul its fleet of standardised post-war buses, while using Chiswick for overhauling the mechanical components received from the garages as well as from the chassis dismantled at Aldenham.

Aldenham was fully commissioned in 1956. London Transport had built for itself the largest bus overhaul works in the world, capable of overhauling 45 buses each week by methods which were a continuation of the constant-flow process developed since the birth of Chiswick. The aim was that once arrived in the works, a bus should always be having something done to it until its departure 15 days later. The first thing to happen was the divorce of body and chassis. When the two, almost certainly not the same two, were reunited before road testing and painting, both had been stripped, checked, cleaned, repaired and renewed, so that the end product, gleaming in its red or green livery in the recertification shop, was just like a brand-new bus.

Among the most spectacular features of Aldenham were the overhead cranes with their lifting capacity of 12 tons, capable of moving complete bus bodies from one end of the works to the other for different tasks to be performed. Aldenham, which was equipped with the most modern body overhaul and painting processes, also had shops for blind making and seat recovering. One of the last stops a bus made on its journey through the works was at the tilt test, where vehicle stability was tested to the maximum: a target of 28° from vertical without tipping over.

Aldenham happily adapted to the task of overhauling the Routemaster, the first examples of which entered the works in 1963. The length of time between overhauls was increased during the 1960s, and a system of vehicle repainting, which did not involve a body/chassis split, was introduced between overhauls. The establishment did not adapt so readily to overhauling the first generation of driver-only buses.

On giving a trial overhaul to a DMS in 1974 it did not prove possible to remove the body from the chassis without causing it serious distortion. Eventually Aldenham was giving overhauls to DMSs and later Metrobuses, Titans and Leyland Nationals, without the usual body lift, but the system necessitated a revision to the time honoured works-flow process.

Another important change in bus maintenance procedure came into effect on 1st April 1981 when the Certificate of Fitness — an essential for every bus — was replaced by the more stringent Freedom from Defect Certificate as required by the EEC. In preparation for this the Aldenham overhaul programme was phased out and replaced by a four-yearly overhaul called a WASP (Works Annual Service Programme). In between WASPs, buses would be subject to a yearly GASP (Garage Annual Service Programme).

In September 1982, following the Law Lords' adverse ruling on the cheap fares policy, mentioned in chapter one, a major slimming down of London's bus services began. It spelt doom for many more crew-operated buses especially in the suburbs, and it spelt doom for Aldenham as well.

RM overhauling involving a complete body lift ceased in 1983. RM overhauls were in any event running down as withdrawals commenced, and London Buses' own tendering exercises were giving a sizeable proportion of bus overhaul work and heavy maintenance to other companies. The decision was taken to close Aldenham and transfer the diminishing overhaul work back to Chiswick.

Aldenham bus overhaul plant finally closed in December 1987 and today lies empty awaiting its fate. But it will never be forgotten so long as television gives us repeat showings of Cliff Richard's 1963 musical film 'Summer Holiday', the first ten minutes of which were filmed in the main works. Perhaps future generations looking at these celluloid images in years to come will marvel at the sheer size and concentration of effort which went into maintaining the largest standardised and unified bus fleet in the world.

As soon as planned Northern Line extensions were abandoned, the depot site near Aldenham was earmarked for a huge bus overhaul works to relieve the pressure on Chiswick. Here in the early 1950s, even before the new complex is completed, a haphazard mixture of buses await attention.
Bruce Jenkins

Aldenham Works was the ultimate in precision and organisation. In its heyday 1,800 staff were employed there and over 50 completely

overhauled buses were despatched each week. A good-as-new RM 188 is seen leaving the Works in 1975. Before its closure, Aldenham Works moved on to deal with the Swifts and Fleetlines purchased in the 1970s, though these did not fit in well with the system for which Aldenham was designed. A Bristol LH is in for accident repair in this 1977 view.
Capital Transport

DEALING WITH DELAYS

The past forty years have witnessed the development of many novel systems designed to keep track of bus movements and position 'in the field'. The first was BESI (Bus Electronic Scanning Indicator). The idea was that each bus on specified routes would have its route and running number coded in a plate fixed to the side of the upper deck. As buses passed special scanners placed at intervals along the route, an electronic eye would read the code on the plate and pass the information to a central control room where it was transmitted onto a screen. Trials with BESI were begun late in 1957 on route 74 and by the mid-1960s BESI was helping to sort out delays on six busy routes including the 6, 9 and 13. However, traffic problems were such that BESI would have had to have been applied to a significant proportion of routes to be really effective and use of the system ceased in 1976. A small-scale experiment in 1972 with 2-way radios linking bus drivers and route controllers was followed in 1973 by CARLA (Computer Assisted Radio Location Aid) which was centred on route 11. With the help of a computer, a centrally based route controller could keep track of each bus by measuring wheel revolutions. CARLA was not very successful and experimentation had ended by 1976.

London Transport did not merely confine its efforts in solving traffic congestion to evaluating sophisticated computer-based systems. By 1976, 200 route inspectors had been issued with pocket radios and many buses had been fitted with radios too. The number had doubled by 1977, by which time 1,500 of LT's buses had been fitted with radios. Bus crews could thus be kept in contact with the central controllers to report unusual traffic conditions and other out-of-course events. The radios were fitted to every London bus by 1987.

By the mid-1980s trials were well under way on the 36 group of routes with BUSCO, another computerised weapon in the battle against traffic delays. BUSCO linked drivers and route controllers who had at their desks a visual display unit showing the scheduled and actual location of all buses on the route. Any gaps in service could thus be detected and remedial action taken. The lack of radio channels led BUSCO designers to use a system of standard coded messages transmitted to display screens fitted in bus cabs. The computer contacted each bus in turn to find out how far it had travelled since passing the last in a series of road loops; it then read any message from the drivers which they could send by pressing one of the function keys on a keyboard in the bus cab. There was a limited two-way speech function. The computer could also send standard messages to the driver such as TURN AT MA (turn at Marble Arch) which remained displayed until the driver touched the ACK (acknowledged) key.

Use of BUSCO has now been phased out, but an interesting by-product of it was PIBS (Passenger Information at Bus Stops). In trials conducted in the Lewisham and New Cross areas starting in August 1986, PIBS told waiting bus passengers what they always wanted to know, how long it would be before the next bus arrived. A screen attached inside the roofs of bus shelters displayed messages like '36B 2 and 7 minutes'.

In May 1992 London Transport unveiled Countdown, real-time passenger information along an entire route, in this case the 18 from Sudbury to King's Cross. Bus drivers enter bus destination details transmitted over radio link to microwave beacons. Wheel turn counters do the rest, sending details of the latest beacon to be passed, and the wheel count, over the radio to a central computer at Westbourne Park garage. The computer estimates waiting times for each stop based on expected journey time and the speed of previous buses. Display panels at bus shelters show a three-line LED giving destination information and arrival times of the next three buses. Countdown is part of a system called Automatic Vehicle Location (AVL) which uses similar beacons to those providing the Countdown information to track the location of buses working on routes 28, 31 and 70, also controlled from Westbourne Park. In this way the service on the three routes can be regulated if delays are causing irregularity.

A K-type open-topper running on London's first all-night bus service in 1923 contrasts with a Metrobus on all-night work in Cockspur Street in 1987.
LT Museum/R.J. Waterhouse

NIGHT BUSES

London's night bus services can be traced back to 1913 when the General introduced night route 94 from Cricklewood to Liverpool Street via Edgware Road, Oxford Street, Regent Street, Strand, Cannon Street, and Bank. There had been some all night tram services since 1901 but the 94, and its sister route the 94A which was introduced later in 1913, were London's very first night bus routes. They were suspended in 1916 because of wartime fuel shortages and did not reappear until 1920. Some night journeys were added to normal daytime routes in 1923 and thereafter the network grew, albeit slowly. By 1934 there were 12 night bus routes, almost all of them north of the Thames, night services in the south being the province of the trams which also continued to run on some north London routes until being replaced by trolleybuses in the late 1930s. Like their daytime contemporaries the night services have been altered down the years with journeys tailored to fit different requirements, largely night workers such as newspapermen and office cleaners, but the basic pattern of service remained unaltered for many years until April 1984 when the whole network was enlarged for a growing leisure market.

The new services proved popular, especially on Friday and Saturday nights when capacity problems were experienced on many of the routes out of central London. There have been frequent additions and alterations since.

TENDERED ROUTES

Since the passing of the 1984 LRT Act, independent companies have been able to tender for the provision of bus services in competition with London Buses Ltd. In the period since the first batch of tendered bus services began operation, the colour of the local bus has changed for thousands of Londoners although in many cases the routes have not altered significantly. When London Buses Ltd was created as a subsidiary of LRT it inherited a virtual operating monopoly of London's bus routes. But the days of a monolithic bus operator for London were effectively over, for the first invitations to tender for selected routes had already been made. London Buses had to take its place in the arena of competition and free enterprise.

The aim of bus route tendering is to make services more efficient and reduce the level of subsidy which the government has to pay in grants. In 1983, its last full year of financial control over London Transport, the Greater London Council contributed a subsidy of £220 million to help run London's buses and the Underground. One of LRT's objectives under the 1984 Act was to reduce the subsidy level by securing the best and most cost-effective services. An initial batch of twelve bus routes was put out to tender in October 1984 and the successful contractors commenced operation the following July.

The tendering process involves prospective contractors submitting a detailed profile of their company, including financial status and available resources, to LRT along with their tender bid. The tender invitations give prospective operators a full service specification drawn up by LRT planners, including duration of the service each day and minimum number of journeys to be operated etc. The choice of vehicle is left to the operator, subject to guidelines from LRT on capacity, destination displays and other detailed design features.

London Buses bid successfully for six of the first batch of twelve tendered services, while LRT estimated that the initial batch of tenders saved 25% of the costs of their operation. The relationship with its contractors enables LRT to maintain close scrutiny of service operation and performance. It is based on LRT paying the operator the full cost of running the service whilst claiming back all the fares taken. This arrangement allows the tendered services to keep within the established fare structure, including the acceptance of the popular Travelcards. To this end LRT supplies the different companies with standard Wayfarer ticket issuing equipment, and the buses working on the tendered services are also subject to ticket inspection by LBL ticket inspectors whether or not LBL is the operating company. LRT stipulate that all buses on tendered routes are fitted with tachographs to enable a check to be kept on mileage. Strict adherence to the timetable, planned by LRT, is essential; persistent early or late running, or not running at all, will result in financial penalties or a contract being terminated.

The first two rounds of tendering consisted entirely of individual routes spread over a wide area, but with the third round LRT changed its tactics and reorganised a network of services in a defined area, in this case Orpington. Before inviting tenders, LRT published details of its plans to local authorities, and to local residents, and invited comments. The proposals were designed to improve local transport within Orpington and to give good links between those new local services and trunk routes to places such as Bromley, the nearest large shopping centre. One feature of the scheme was a midibus network penetrating many areas which had not previously had a bus service, and stretching across the London border down into Kent. London Buses formed a subsidiary company, Orpington Buses, trading as ROUNDABOUT, which tendered en bloc for the midibus routes numbered R1-R6. The bid was successful and the maroon and grey Iveco and Optare/Volkswagen City Pacer minibuses soon became a familiar and popular sight in suburban Kent and down into the Weald. Other low-cost units followed in the Bexleyheath, Harrow, Kingston, Sutton and Stanwell areas of suburban London. Of these only Stanwell Buses, trading as Westlink, remains as a separate operation.

A pioneer of the independent era in central London was Grey-Green, whose Volvo Citybuses are still a familiar sight on route 24 in 1994. Number 125 in the Grey-Green fleet is at Mornington Crescent in October 1989.
Martin Ruthe

Capital Citybus Leyland bodied Olympian number 143 passes through Gidea Park in October 1992 bearing the vivid yellow and red livery now common throughout north and east London where the company has successfully tendered for many LT services.
Martin Ruthe

1988 provided a landmark when the 24 became the first trunk central London bus route to be won on tender by a non-LBL bidder. The lucky winner was Grey-Green whose Volvo Citybuses soon became a prominent sight in a still predominantly sea of bus red. Grey-Green's lone position was short lived. London & Country subsequently won tenders for routes 78 and 176 and Kentish Bus the 19, 22A and 22B, all penetrating the central area. The 19 was of note because it was the first crew-operated route to be tendered on the basis that the vehicles, refurbished RMLs, would be supplied by LRT to the successful bidder in the appropriate livery. Kentish Bus began its route 19 contract in April 1993. In December 1993 route 13 became the second crew route to be contracted to a non-LBL bidder, in this case BTS of Borehamwood who likewise received a batch of newly modernised RMLs clad in the BTS light red and yellow livery. An unusual feature of this contract is that BTS's RMLs run on Sundays, the first crew buses to operate in the capital on this day since 1988.

Elsewhere, new network schemes and route tendering exercises have continued unabated since the process of competitive tendering began in 1985, so that by the end of the 1992/93 financial year London Transport was able to report that 44 per cent of London's bus route network was being operated under contract. The start of the process in the mid-1980s resulted in most of the London bus network outside the Greater London boundary being contracted out as part of joint LRT/County exercises, with the result that red buses are rarely seen across the London border.

It is the network schemes which have brought the mini and midibuses into their own. Generally minibus routes operate at higher frequencies than the 'big bus' services they replace. Small buses are at the sharp end of the marketing effort in the new age of bus operation, aimed at strengthening the role of the bus in the community. Many appear on new route networks adorned with names like Hoppa, Skipper, Streetline and Midilink, penetrating previously busless areas. Also they are friendly and convenient, particularly in the eyes of the elderly who make up a sizeable proportion of London's bus travellers. They herald a new age in London bus travel.

But for an established operator like London Buses, with carefully negotiated rates of pay and conditions for staff, a successful bid against other hopeful operators for a minibus route usually means lower pay scales and altered working conditions. This has caused problems on the industrial relations front, the most serious of which saw the demise of LBL subsidiary London Forest in 1991 following a series of strikes arising out of new wage rate proposals, essential if the unit was to manage the operation of the routes in the new Walthamstow bus network it had won on competitive tender.

This setback apart, London Buses has fared reasonably well in the new commercial environment. It has tapped lucrative new markets in areas as diverse as the provision of commuter expresses, the successful 'Airbus' services to Heathrow, and bargain hunters' services to superstores and big shopping complexes like Brent Cross and even Lakeside on the Essex marshes; and it has won routes on competitive tender. The successes have not been without sacrifice and cost economies. When routes have been lost, remaining operations have been rationalised and as a result many garages have been closed. It is the era of the 'greenfield' site, with buses kept in the open with the minimum of essential on-site staff and maintenance facilities. Such operations are commonplace amongst independent companies working London bus routes.

In November 1993 the Government announced a deferment of the planned deregulation of London's bus services originally intended for late 1994. The announcement assured the role of London Transport as custodian and planner of London's bus services until at least 1996. However LRT's plans for the privatisation of the London Buses units in 1994 is set to continue.

The face of London's buses in another five years will be very different from its face today, which in turn represents enormous change over that of five years ago. That the debate on whether the change has been one for the better will continue in the future is certainly more easy to predict.